QUESTIONS AND ANSWERS

TO THE SIX PARTS OF THE

SMALL CATECHISM

OF

DR. MARTIN LUTHER.

Translated from the Fourth Edition of the House-
School- and Church-Book for Christians of the
Lutheran Faith, of

PASTOR WILHELM LOEHE

BY

EDWARD T. HORN, D. D.

COLUMBIA, S. C.:
W. J. DUFFIE.

Windham Press is committed to bringing the lost cultural heritage of ages past into the 21st century through high-quality reproductions of original, classic printed works at affordable prices.

This book has been carefully crafted to utilize the original images of antique books rather than error-prone OCR text. This also preserves the work of the original typesetters of these classics, unknown craftsmen who laid out the text, often by hand, of each and every page you will read. Their subtle art involving judgment and interaction with the text is in many ways superior and more human than the mechanical methods utilized today, and gave each book a unique, hand-crafted feel in its text that connected the reader organically to the art of bindery and book-making.

We think these benefits are worth the occasional imperfection resulting from the age of these books at the time of scanning, and their vintage feel provides a connection to the past that goes beyond the mere words of the text.

As bibliophiles, we are always seeking perfection in our work, so please notify us of any errors in this book by emailing us at corrections@windhampress.com. Our team is motivated to correct errors quickly so future customers are better served. Our mission is to raise the bar of quality for reprinted works by a focus on detail and quality over mass production. To peruse our catalog of carefully curated classic works, please visit our online store at www.windhampress.com.

TRANSLATOR'S PREFACE.

IN the successive prefaces to the four editions of his Explanation of the Catechism, Löhe says that he prepared it first of all for the use of scattered Lutherans in America. It is a part of his Book for the House, School and Church. As he says in his *Three Books on the Church*, "House, School and Church are made one Church by our precious Catechism." In this translation I have incorporated only the *Definitions*, the *Explanation* and the *Questions about the Bible;* omitting the *Proof-texts* and the *Questions for one about to go to the Holy Supper*, for which I would refer to *Luther's Small Catechism with Scripture Texts*, published by The Lutheran Bookstore, Philadelphia.

Doubtless there are many excellent explanations of the Catechism by approved teachers. The excellence of *this* explanation is, that it attempts no more than to analyze and explain Luther's Catechism itself. It does not try to find in it the whole scheme of doctrine. It is intended, like Luther's Catechism, to show a house-father how to teach his household. "The father, the children, the household, should use, pray, learn, prize it; and so it will become the cruse of the woman of Sarepta, in which the oil never fails."

I find reason to criticise this excellent book only in

those particulars in which the author seems to me to have gone beyond his purpose, and added to Luther's Catechism; but I thought it right, and most helpful to the Church, to give as faithfully as I can the author's whole explanation. In conclusion, let me join him in asking those called to teach, to read Luther's advice in his Prefaces to his two Catechisms.

ENCHIRIDION.

THE
SMALL CATECHISM

OF

DR. MARTIN LUTHER

FOR

PASTORS AND PREACHERS

PREFACE OF DR. MARTIN LUTHER.

Martin Luther to all faithful and godly pastors and preachers, Grace, Mercy and Peace, in Jesus Christ our Lord!

THE deplorable condition in which I found religious affairs during a recent visitation of the congregations, has impelled me to publish this Catechism, or statement of the Christian doctrine, after having prepared it in very brief and simple terms. Alas! what misery I beheld! The people, especially those who live in the villages, seem to have no knowledge whatever of Christian doctrine, and many of the pastors are ignorant and incompetent teachers. And, nevertheless, they all maintain that they are Christians, that they have been baptized, and that they have received the Lord's Supper. Yet they cannot recite the Lord's Prayer, the Creed, or the Ten Commandments; they live as if they were irrational creatures, and now that the Gospel has come to them, they grossly abuse their Christian liberty.

Ye bishops! what answer will ye give to Christ for having so shamefully neglected the people, and paid no attention to the duties of your office? I invoke no evil on your heads. But you withhold the cup in the Lord's Supper, insist on the observance of your human laws, and yet, at the same time, do not take the least interest in teaching the people the Lord's Prayer, the Creed, the Ten Commandments, or any other part of the Word of God. Woe unto you!

Wherefore I beseech you in the Name of God, my beloved brethren, who are pastors or preachers, to engage heartily in the discharge of the duties of your office, to have mercy on the people who are entrusted to your care, and to assist us in introducing the Catechism among them, and especially among the young. And if any of you do not possess the necessary qualifications, I beseech you to take at least the following forms, and read them, word for word, to the people, on this wise:—

In the first place; let the preacher take the utmost care to avoid all changes or variations in the text and wording of the Ten Commandments, the Lord's Prayer, the Creed, the Sacraments, etc. Let him, on the contrary, take each of the forms respectively, adhere to it and repeat it anew, year after year. For young and inexperienced people cannot be successfully instructed, unless we adhere to the same text or the same forms of expression. They easily become confused, when the teacher at one time employs a certain form of words and expressions, and, at another, apparently with a view to make improvements, adopts a different form. The result of such a course will be, that all the time and labor which we have expended will be lost.

This point was well understood by our venerable fathers, who were accustomed to use the same words in teaching the Lord's Prayer, the Creed, and the Ten Commandments. We, too, should follow this plan when we teach these things, particularly in the case of the young and ignorant, not changing a single syllable, nor introducing any variations when, year after year, we recur to these forms and recite them anew before our hearers.

Choose, therefore, the form of words which best pleases you, and adhere to it perpetually. When you preach in the presence of intelligent and learned men, you are at liberty to exhibit your knowledge and skill, and may present and discuss these subjects in all the varied modes which are at your command. But when you are teaching the young, retain the same form and manner without change; teach them, first of all, the Ten Commandments, the Creed, the Lord's Prayer, etc., always presenting the same words of the text, so that those who learn can repeat them after you, and retain them in the memory.

But if any refuse to receive your instructions, tell them plainly that they deny Christ and are not Christians; such persons shall not be admitted to the Lord's Table, nor present a child for Baptism, nor enjoy any of our Christian privileges, but are to be sent back to the pope and his agents, and indeed, to Satan himself. Their parents and employers should, besides, refuse to furnish them with food and drink, and notify them that the government was disposed to banish from the country all persons of such a rude and intractable character.

For although we cannot, and should not, compel

them to exercise faith, we ought, nevertheless, to instruct the great mass with all diligence, so that they may know how to distinguish between right and wrong in their conduct towards those with whom they live, or among whom they desire to earn their living. For whoever desires to reside in a city, and enjoy the rights and privileges which its laws confer, is also bound to know and obey those laws. God grant that such persons may become sincere believers! But if they remain dishonest and vicious, let them at least withhold from public view the vices of their hearts.

In the second place; when those whom you are instructing have become familiar with the words of the text, it is time to teach them to understand the meaning of those words, so that they may become acquainted with the object and purport of the lesson. Then proceed to another of the following forms, or, at your pleasure, choose any other which is brief, and adhere strictly to the same words and forms of expression in the text, without altering a single syllable; besides, allow yourself ample time for the lessons. For it is not necessary that you should, on the same occasion, proceed from the beginning to the end of the several parts; it will be more profitable if you present them separately, in regular succession. When the people have, for instance, at length correctly understood the First Commandment, you may proceed to the Second, and so continue. By neglecting to observe this mode, the people will be overburdened, and be prevented from understanding and retaining in memory any considerable part of the matter communicated to them.

In the third place; when you have thus reached the end of this short Catechism, begin anew with the Large Catechism, and by means of it furnish the people with fuller and more comprehensive explanations. Explain here at large every Commandment, every Petition, and, indeed, every part, showing the duties which they severally impose, and both the advantages which follow the performance of those duties, and also the dangers and losses which result from the neglect of them. Insist in an especial manner on such Commandments or other parts as seem to be most of all misunderstood or neglected by your people. It will, for example, be necessary that you should enforce with the utmost earnestness the Seventh Commandment, which treats of Stealing, when you are teaching workmen, dealers, and even farmers and servants, inasmuch as many of these are guilty of various dishonest and thievish practices. So, too, it will be your duty to explain and apply the Fourth Commandment with great diligence, when you are teaching children and uneducated adults, and to urge them to observe order, to be faithful, obedient and peaceable, as well as to adduce numerous instances mentioned in the Scriptures, which show that God punished such as were guilty in these things, and blessed the obedient.

Here, too, let it be your great aim to urge magistrates and parents to rule wisely, and to educate the children, admonishing them, at the same time, that such duties are imposed on them, and showing them how grievously they sin if they neglect them. For in such a case they overthrow and lay waste alike the kingdom of God and the kingdom of the world, acting as if they were the worst enemies both of God and of man. And show them very plainly the shocking evils of which they are the authors, when they refuse their aid in training up children to be pastors, preachers, writers, etc., and set forth that on account of such sins God will inflict an awful punishment upon them. It is indeed, necessary to preach on these things; for parents and magistrates are guilty of sins in this respect, which are so great that there are no terms in which they can be described. And truly, Satan has a cruel design in fostering these evils.

Finally; inasmuch as the people are now relieved from the tyranny of the pope, they refuse to come to the Lord's Table, and treat it with contempt. On this point, also, it is very necessary that you should give them instructions, while, at the same time, you are to be guided by the following principles: That we are to compel no one to believe, or to receive the Lord's Supper; that we are not to establish any laws on this point, or appoint the time and place; but that we should so preach as to influence the people, without any law adopted by us, to urge, and, as it were, to compel us who are pastors, to administer the Lord's Supper to them. Now this object may be attained, if we address them in the following manner: It is to be feared that he who does not desire to receive the Lord's Supper at least three or four times during the year, despises the Sacrament, and is no Christian. So, too, he is no Christian, who neither believes nor obeys the Gospel; for Christ did not say: "Omit, or despise this," but, "This do ye, as oft as ye drink it," etc. He commands that this should be done, and by no means be neglected and despised. He says: "This do."

Now he who does not highly value the Sacrament, shows thereby that he has no sin, no flesh, no devil, no world, no death, no danger, no hell; that is to say, he does not believe that such evils exist, although he may be deeply immersed in them, and completely belong to the devil. On the other hand, he needs no grace, no life, no Paradise, no heaven, no Christ, no God, no good thing. For if he believed that he was involved in such evils, and that he was in need of such blessings, he could not refrain from receiving the Sacrament, wherein aid is afforded against such evils, and, again, such blessings are bestowed. It will not be necessary to compel him by the force of any law to approach the Lord's Table; he will hasten to it of his own accord, will compel himself to come, and indeed urge you to administer the Sacrament to him.

Hence, you are by no means to adopt any compulsory law in this case, as the pope has done. Let it simply be your aim to set forth distinctly the advantages and losses, the wants and the benefits, the dangers and the blessings, which are to be considered in connection with the Sacrament; the people will, doubtless, then seek it without urgent demands on your part. If they still refuse to come forward, let them choose their own ways, and tell them that those who do not regard their own spiritual misery, and do not desire the gracious help of God, belong to Satan.

But if you do not give such solemn admonitions, or if you adopt odious compulsory laws on the subject, it is your own fault if the people treat the Sacrament with contempt. Will they not necessarily be slothful, if you are silent and sleep? Therefore consider the subject seriously, ye Pastors and Preachers! Our office has now assumed a very different character from that which it bore under the pope; it is now of a very grave nature, and is very salutary in its influence. It consequently subjects us to far greater burdens and labors, dangers and temptations, while it brings with it an inconsiderable reward, and very little gratitude in the world. But Christ Himself will be our reward, if we labor with fidelity. May He grant such mercy unto us who is the Father of all grace, to whom be given thanks and praises through Christ our Lord, for ever! Amen.

WITTENBERG, A. D. 1529.

I.
THE TEN COMMANDMENTS.

In the plain form in which the head of the family should teach them to his household.

I AM THE LORD THY GOD.

The First Commandment.

Thou shalt have no other gods before me.

Thou shalt not make unto thee any graven image, or any likeness of anything that is in heaven above, or that is in the earth beneath, or that is in the water under the earth; thou shalt not bow down thyself to them, nor serve them: for I the Lord thy God am a jealous God, visiting the iniquity of the fathers upon the children unto the third and fourth generation of them that hate me; and showing mercy unto thousands of them that love me, and keep my commandments.

Q. What is meant by this?

Ans. We should fear, love and trust in God above all things.

The Second Commandment.

Thou shalt not take the name of the Lord thy God in vain; for the Lord will not hold him guiltless that taketh His name in vain.[1]

Q. What is meant by this?

A. We should fear and love God, and not curse,[2]

---

[1] That is, to use it otherwise than God meant it to be used.
[2] To wish some evil to be done by the Lord.

swear,[3] use witchcraft,[4] lie[5] or deceive[6] by His name, but call upon His name in every time of need, and worship Him with prayer,[7] praise[8] and thanksgiving.[9]

The Third Commandment.

Remember the sabbath day[10] to keep it holy.[11]

Six days shalt thou labor, and do all thy work, but the seventh day is the Sabbath of the Lord thy God: in it thou shalt not do any work, thou, nor thy son, nor thy daughter, thy manservant, nor thy maidservant, nor thy cattle, nor thy stranger that is within thy gates: for in six days the Lord made heaven and earth, the sea, and all that in them is, and rested the seventh day; wherefore the Lord blessed the Sabbath day, and hallowed it.

Q. What is meant by this?

A. We should fear and love God, and not despise preaching and His Word, but keep it holy[12] and gladly hear and learn it.

The Fourth Commandment.

Honor[13] thy father and thy mother, that it may be well with thee, and thou mayest live long on the earth.

Q. What is meant by this?

A. We should fear and love God, and not despise

---

[3] To call God as a witness.
[4] To employ God's Name (Word or creature) by aid of the devil, to find out what God has hidden, or to get what He has withheld
[5] To falsify God's Word and truth.
[6] If the lie is believed by another to his injury.
[7] To ask of God.
[8] To tell God's wonderful qualities and works.
[9] To acknowledge and confess God's good gifts.
[10] Day of rest. In *Hebrew*, Sabbath; in *German*, Feiertag.
[11] To separate it from common, everyday use, and give it to the service of God.
[12] Keep it as God's word, i. e., as unlike every other word, and exalted above every word.
[13] To respect the dignity which God has given to each, and to esteem him accordingly.

our parents and masters, nor provoke them to anger, but honor,[14] serve,[15] obey,[16] love and esteem them.

The Fifth Commandment.

Thou shalt not kill.

Q. What is meant by this?

A. We should fear and love God, and not hurt nor harm our neighbor[17] in his body, but help[18] and befriend[19] him in every bodily need.

The Sixth Commandment.

Thou shalt not commit adultery.[20]

Q. What is meant by this?

A. We should fear and love God, and live chaste[21] and pure[22] in words and deeds, each one loving and honoring his spouse.

The Seventh Commandment.

Thou shalt not steal.

Q What is meant by this?

A. We should fear and love God and not take[23] our neighbor's money or property, nor get it by false wares or dealing, but help him to improve and protect his property and living.

The Eighth Commandment.

Thou shalt not bear false witness against thy neighbor.

---

[14] Show in all our behaviour, that we honour them in our hearts.
[15] In every way even without bidding, to do as pleases them.
[16] To heed their bidding and do it.
[17] Our fellowman, whom it is in our power to help.
[18] Relieve him from need.
[19] Further him.
[20] To break the love and fidelity promised to wife or husband.
[21] To try to keep one's own body and soul free from evil lust.
[22] By neither word nor deed giving another an occasion of evil lust, but rather moving all to a pure and holy life by our example.
[23] That is, wrongfully.

Q. What is meant by this?

A. We should fear and love God, and not falsely[24] belie,[25] betray,[26] slander[27] nor defame[28] our neighbor, but excuse[29] him, speak well[30] of him, and make the best[31] of all he does.

The Ninth Commandment.

Thou shalt not covet thy neighbor's house.

Q. What is meant by this?

A. We should fear and love God, and not craftily seek to gain our neighbor's inheritance or home, nor get it by a show of right, but help and serve him in keeping it.

The Tenth Commandment.

Thou shalt not covet thy neighbor's wife, nor his man-servant, nor his maid-servant, nor his cattle, nor anything that is his.

Q. What is meant by this?

A. We should fear and love God, and not estrange, force[32] or entice[33] away from our neighbor his wife, servants or cattle, but urge them to stay and do their duty.

Q. What does God say of all these commandments?

A. He says: I the Lord thy God am a jealous[34] God, visiting[35] the iniquity of the fathers upon the

---

[24] Out of a false heart.
[25] To lie against our neighbor.
[26] To tell our neighbour's secret to his harm.
[27] To lie against him behind his back.
[28] To raise bad reports.
[29] Defend him against unjust blame.
[30] If others speak of him only evil, forgetting the good that may be said.
[31] Put the best explanation on what he does or does not.
[32] Leave him no peace, until he gives.
[33] To take away their heart and confidence from husband or master.
[34] Who strictly requires the love we owe Him.
[35] In order to punish.

children unto the third and fourth generation of them that hate me; and showing mercy unto thousands of them that love me and keep my commandments.

Q. What is meant by this?

God threatens to punish all who transgress these commandments; therefore we should fear His wrath, and do nothing against such commandments. But He promises grace and every blessing to all who keep these commandments; therefore we should love and trust in Him, and gladly do according to His commandments.

II.

THE CREED.[1]

In the plain form in which the head of the family should teach it to his household.

The First Article.[2]
Of Creation.

I believe in God the Father Almighty, Maker of heaven and earth.

Q. What is meant by this?

A. I believe that God has made[3] me, together with all creatures;[4] that He has given and still preserves to me my body and soul, eyes, ears, and all my members, my reason and all my senses; also clothing and shoes, meat and drink, house and home, wife and child, land, cattle and all my goods; that He richly and daily provides me with all that I need for this body and life, protects[5] me against all danger, and keeps me and guards me from all evil; and all this purely out of fatherly, divine goodness and mercy, without any

---

[1] Statement and confession of what we believe and ought to believe.
[2] Member. Part.
[3] Out of nothing.
[4] All things made.
[5] Covers me, so that I am safe.

merit or worthiness in me; for all which I am in duty bound to thank and praise, to serve and obey Him. This is most certainly true.

The Second Article.
Of Redemption.

And in Jesus[6] Christ[7] His only Son, our Lord, who was conceived by the Holy Ghost, born of the Virgin Mary; suffered under Pontius Pilate,[8] was crucified, dead and buried; He descended into hell; the third day He rose again from the dead; He ascended into heaven, and sitteth on the right hand of God the Father Almighty; from thence He shall come to judge[9] the quick and the dead.

Q. What is meant by this?

A. I believe that Jesus Christ, true God, begotten of the Father from eternity, and also true man, born of the Virgin Mary, is my Lord; who has redeemed[10] me, a lost and condemned creature, purchased[11] and won[12] me from all sins, from death, and from the power of the devil, not with gold or silver, but with His holy, precious blood, and with His innocent sufferings and death: in order that I might be His own, live under Him in His kingdom, and serve Him in everlasting righteousness, innocence and blessedness, even as He is risen from the dead, lives and reigns[13] to all eternity. This is most certainly true.

The Third Article.
Of Sanctification.

I believe in the Holy Ghost; the holy Christian

---

[6] Saviour.
[7] Messiah, the Anointed One.
[8] The Governor of Judea, appointed by the Roman Emperor.
[9] To distinguish and separate the bad from the good.
[10] Ransomed.
[11] Earned me by His labour. Bought me with a price.
[12] In battle.
[13] As a king.

Church,[14] the Communion of Saints; the Forgiveness of sins; the Resurrection of the body; and the Life everlasting. Amen.[15]

Q. What is meant by this?

A. I believe that I cannot by my own reason or strength believe in Jesus Christ my Lord, or come to Him; but the Holy Ghost has called[16] me by the Gospel,[17] enlightened[18] me with His gifts, and sanctified and preserved me in the true faith; even as He calls, gathers, enlightens, and sanctifies the whole Christian Church on earth, and preserves it in union with Jesus Christ in the one true faith; in which Christian Church He daily and richly forgives me and all believers all our sins, and at the last day[19] will raise up me and all the dead, and will grant me and all believers in Christ everlasting life. This is most certainly true.

III.

THE LORD'S PRAYER.

In the plain form in which the head of the family should teach it to his household.

Our Father who art in heaven.

Q. What is meant by this?

A. God would hereby tenderly invite us to believe that He is truly our Father, and we are truly His children, so that we may ask of Him with all cheerfulness and confidence, as dear children of their dear father.

---

[14] A spiritual Temple of the Lord, built of living stones, in which He dwelleth.
[15] This is most certainly true.
[16] To summon from one place to another.
[17] The good tidings of the forgiveness of sins for the sake of the sufferings and death Christ bore in our stead.
[18] To give light or knowledge.
[19] The last day of the world.

The First Petition.

Hallowed be Thy name.

Q. What is meant by this?

A. The name of God is indeed holy in itself; but we pray in this petition that it may be hallowed also among us.

Q. How is this done?

A. When the Word of God is taught in its truth and purity, and we as the children of God, lead holy lives, in accordance with it; this grant us, dear Father in heaven! But he that teaches and lives otherwise than the Word of God teaches, profanes the name of God among us: from this preserve us, Heavenly Father!

The Second Petition.

Thy kingdom come.

Q. What is meant by this?

A. The kingdom of God comes indeed of itself, without our prayer; but we pray in this petition that it may come also to us.

Q. How is this done?

A. When our heavenly Father gives us His Holy Spirit, so that by His grace we believe His holy Word, and live godly here in time, and in heaven forever.

The Third Petition.

Thy will be done on earth, as it is in heaven.

Q. What is meant by this?

A. The good and gracious will of God is done indeed without our prayer; but we pray in this petition that it may be done also among us.

Q. How is this done?

A. When God breaks and hinders every evil counsel and purpose, which would not let us hallow God's name nor let His kingdom come, such as the will of

THE LORD'S PRAYER.

the devil, the world, and our own flesh; but strengthens and keeps us steadfast in His Word and in faith unto our end. This is His gracious and good will.

The Fourth Petition.

Give us this day our daily bread.

Q. What is meant by this?

A. God gives daily bread indeed without our prayer even to all the wicked; but we pray in this petition that He would lead us to acknowledge and receive our daily bread with thanksgiving.

Q. What is meant by "daily bread"?

A. All that belongs to the wants and support of the body, such as meat, drink, clothing, shoes, house, home, land, cattle, money, goods, a pious spouse, pious children, pious servants, pious and faithful rulers, good government, good weather, peace, health, order, honor, good friends, trusty neighbors and the like.

The Fifth Petition.

And forgive us our trespasses as we forgive those who trespass against us.

Q. What is meant by this?

A. We pray in this petition that our Father in heaven would not look upon our sins, nor, on account of them, deny our prayer; for we are not worthy of anything we ask, neither have we deserved it; but that He would grant us all through grace; for we sin much every day, and deserve nothing but punishment. And we on our part will heartily forgive and readily do good to those who sin against us.

The Sixth Petition.

And lead us not into temptation.

Q. What is meant by this?

A. God indeeds tempts[1] no one, but we pray in this petition that God would guard and keep us, that the devil, the world and our flesh[2] may not deceive us, nor lead us into misbelief,[3] despair[4] and other shameful sin and vice; and, though we be thus tempted,[5] that we may still in the end overcome, and have the victory.

The Seventh Petition.

But deliver us from evil.

Q. What is meant by this?

A. We pray in this petition, as the sum of all, that our Father in heaven would deliver us from all manner of evil—in body and soul, property and honor—and at last, when the hour of death shall come, grant us a blessed end, and graciously take us from this vale of sorrow to himself in heaven.

For Thine is the kingdom and the power and the glory for ever and ever. Amen.

Q. What is meant by this?

A. That I am to be sure that these petitions are acceptable to our Father in heaven, and are heard; for He Himself has commanded us so to pray, and has promised to hear us. Amen, Amen, that is, Yea, Yea; it shall be so.

---

[1] Puts no one to the test, in order to bring him to sin.
[2] Our inborn sinful nature.
[3] A false belief.
[4] Ceasing to doubt, but yielding to unbelief.
[5] Brought into such inward battle.

IV.

THE SACRAMENT[1] OF HOLY BAPTISM.

In the plain form in which the head of the family should teach it to his household.

I.

Q. What is Baptism?

A. Baptism is not simply water, but it is the water comprehended in God's command, and connected with God's word.

Q. What is that word of God?

A. That which Christ our Lord says in the last chapter of Matthew: "Go ye and teach all nations, baptizing them in the name of the Father, and of the Son, and of the Holy Ghost."

II.

Q. What benefits does Baptism confer?

A. It works forgiveness of sins, delivers from death and the devil, and gives everlasting salvation to all who believe what the words and promises of God declare.

Q. Which are those words and promises of God?

A. Those which Christ our Lord says in the last chapter of Mark: "He that believeth and is baptized shall be saved; but he that believeth not, shall be damned."

III.

Q. How can water do such great things?

A. It is not water indeed that does it, but the word of God, which is in and with the water, and faith which trusts this word of God in the water. For without the word of God, the water is simply water, and no baptism; but with the word of God, it is a baptism, that is, a gracious water of life and a washing

---

[1] A holy mystery.

of regeneration in the Holy Ghost; as St.[2] Paul says, Titus iii. 5–8: "According to His mercy He saved us, by the washing of regeneration, and renewing of the Holy Ghost; which He shed on us abundantly through Jesus Christ our Saviour; that being justified by His grace, we should be made heirs according to the hope of eternal life. This is a faithful saying."

IV.

Q. What does such baptizing with water signify?

A. It signifies that the old Adam[3] in us should, by daily sorrow and repentance, be drowned and die, with all sins and evil lusts; and, again, a new man daily come forth and arise, who shall live before God in righteousness and purity for ever.

Q. Where is this written?

A. St. Paul says, Rom. vi. 4: "We are buried with Christ by baptism into death; that like as He was raised up from the dead by the glory of the Father, even so we also should walk in newness of life."

OF THE OFFICE OF THE KEYS AND CONFESSION.

A.

(*From the Kinderpredigten of the Brandenburg-Nürnberg Order of 1533.*)

Q. What word of God belongs to the Office of the Keys?

A. Jesus breathed on His disciples, and said unto them, Receive ye the Holy Ghost: whosesoever sins ye remit, they are remitted unto them; and whosoever sins ye retain, they are retained. John xx. 22, 23.

Q. What is meant by this?

I believe that what the called ministers of Christ do to us by His divine commandment, especially when they shut open and impenitent sinners out of the Fellowship of the Christian Church, and absolve those who repent of their sin and intend to amend, is as valid and certain even in Heaven, as if our Lord Jesus Christ did it Himself.

---

[2] *I. e.*, the holy Paul.
[3] The sinful nature born in us.

B.

HOW PEOPLE SHOULD BE TAUGHT TO CONFESS.

Q. What is Confession?

A. Confession embraces two parts: one, that we confess our sins; the other, that we receive absolution or forgiveness from the pastor as from God Himself and in no wise doubt, but firmly believe that through it our sins are forgiven before God in heaven.

Q. What sins should we confess?

A. Before God we should acknowledge ourselves guilty of all sins, even of those which we do not discern; as we do in the Lord's Prayer. But before the pastor we should confess those sins only which we know and feel in our hearts.

Q. Which are these?

A. Here consider your station in the light of the Ten Commandments: whether you be a father, mother, son, daughter, master, mistress, servant; whether you have been disobedient, unfaithful, slothful; whether you have wronged any one by word or deed; whether you have stolen, neglected, wasted aught, done any harm.

Q. Please show me a short way to confess?

A. You should say, Reverend and dear sir, I beseech you to hear my confession, and to announce to me forgiveness for God's sake.

Say,

I, a poor sinner, confess before God that I am guilty of all sins; especially before thee I confess that I am a man-servant, a maid-servant, etc.; but I have been unfaithful to my master; in this case or in that I have not done what he bade me; I have provoked him and caused him to curse; I have neglected many things and let them go to waste; in words and deeds I have been immodest; I have been angry with my fellows; I have grumbled and sworn at my wife, etc. For all this I am sorry and ask forgiveness. I mean to do better.

A Master or Mistress should say thus:

In particular I confess before thee that I have not been faithful in training my children, domestics, family, to God's glory. I have cursed. I have set a bad example by unchaste words and deeds. I have injured my neighbour. I have slandered, have overcharged, or given false goods, or false measure. And whatever more he may have done in violation of God's commandment.

If any one do not feel oppressed by such or greater sins, let him not be anxious, or hunt up and invent sins, and thereby make his confession a torture, but let him name the one or two sins he knows. Thus: In particular, I confess that once I cursed. Once I used immodest words. I have neglected this or that, etc. This is enough.

But if you know of none at all (which is hardly possible), mention none in particular, but receive the forgiveness after the General Confession which you make before God to the minister.

Then the Confessor should say:

God be merciful unto thee and strengthen thy faith. Amen.

And

Dost thou believe that my forgiveness is the forgiveness of God? *A.* Yes, dear sir.

Then let him say,

As thou believest, so be it done unto thee. And in the Name of our Lord Jesus Christ I forgive thee thy sins, in the Name of the Father, and of the Son, and of the Holy Ghost. Amen. Depart in peace.

A pastor will know how to console with passages of Scripture those who have great burdens on their conscience, or are distressed and tempted, and can encourage them to believe. The form just given is intended only as a pattern for the simple.

V.

THE SACRAMENT OF THE ALTAR.[1]

In the plain form in which the head of the family should teach it to his household.

Q. What is the Sacrament of the altar?

A. It is the true body and blood of our Lord Jesus Christ, under the bread and wine, instituted by Christ Himself for us Christians to eat and to drink.

---

[1] A table of wood or stone, on which the Holy Supper is made ready, and at which we bring to God an offering of prayer.

SACRAMENT OF THE ALTAR.

Q. Where is this written?

A. The holy Evangelists,[2] Matthew, Mark and Luke, together with St. Paul, write thus:

"Our Lord Jesus Christ, the same night in which He was betrayed, took bread: and when He had given thanks, He brake it, and gave it to His disciples, and said, Take eat; this is my body, which is given for you: this do in remembrance of me.

"After the same manner also He took the cup, when He had supped, gave thanks, and gave it to them, saying, Take and drink ye all of it: this cup is the new testament in my blood, which is shed for you, for the remission of sins: this do ye, as oft as ye drink it, in remembrance of me."

Q. Of what use is such eating and drinking?

A. It is shown us by these words: "Given and shed for you, for the remission of sins"; namely, that in the Sacrament forgiveness of sins, life and salvation are given us through these words. For where there is forgiveness of sins, there is also life and salvation.

Q. How can bodily eating and drinking do such great things?

A. It is not the eating and drinking, indeed, that does it, but the words which stand here: "Given and shed for you, for the remission of sins." These words which accompany the bodily eating and drinking, are the chief thing in the Sacrament; and he that believes these words, has what they declare and mean, namely, the forgiveness of sins.

Q. Who then receives this Sacrament worthily?

A. Fasting and bodily preparation are indeed a good[3] outward discipline; but he is truly worthy and well-prepared, who has faith in these words: "Given and shed for you, for the remission of sins." But he

---

[2] The four holy men who have written the life of Christ for us, Matthew, Mark, Luke and John.
[3] Proper and becoming.

who believes not these words, or doubts,[4] is unworthy and unprepared; for the words, FOR YOU, require truly believing hearts.

How the head of the family should teach his household to pray, morning and evening.

Morning Prayer.

In the morning, when thou risest, thou shalt sign thyself with the holy cross, and say:

In the Name of the Father, and of the Son, and of the Holy Ghost. *Amen.*

Then, kneeling or standing, repeat the *Creed*, and the *Lord's Prayer*.

Then mayest thou also say this prayer:

I GIVE thanks unto Thee, Heavenly Father, through Jesus Christ, Thy dear Son, that Thou hast protected me through the night from all danger and harm; and I beseech Thee to preserve and keep me, this day also, from all sin and evil: that in all my thoughts, words, and deeds, I may serve and please Thee. Into Thy hands I commend my body and soul, and all that is mine. Let Thy holy angel have charge concerning me, that the wicked one have no power over me. *Amen.*

Then after a hymn, or the Ten Commandments, or whatever thy devotion may suggest, go joyfully to thy work.

Evening Prayer.

In the evening, when thou goest to bed, thou shalt sign thyself with the holy cross, and say:

In the Name of the Father, and of the Son, and of the Holy Ghost. Amen.

Then, kneeling or standing, thou shalt say the *Creed* and the *Lord's Prayer*.

Then mayest thou say this Prayer:

I GIVE thanks unto Thee, Heavenly Father, through Jesus Christ Thy dear Son, that Thou hast this day so graciously protected me, and I beseech Thee to for-

---

[4] Wavering between belief and unbelief.

give me all my sins, and the wrong which I have done, and by thy great mercy defend me from all the perils and dangers of this night. Into Thy hands I commend my body and soul, and all that is mine. Let Thy holy angel have charge concerning me, that the wicked one have no power over me. *Amen.*

Then lie down in peace and sleep.

How the head of a family should teach his household to ask a blessing and return thanks.

Grace before Meat.

The children and servants shall go to the table reverently, fold their hands and say:

The eyes of all wait upon Thee, O Lord; and Thou givest them their meat in due season. Thou openest Thine hand, and satisfiest the desire[1] of every living thing.

Then shall be said the *Lord's Prayer*, and after that this *Prayer:*

O Lord God, Heavenly Father, bless us and these Thy gifts, which we receive from Thy loving-kindness, through Jesus Christ our Lord. Amen.

Thanks after Meat.

After meat, they shall reverently and with folded hands say:

O GIVE thanks unto the Lord, for He is good: for His mercy endureth forever. He giveth food to all flesh: He giveth to the beast his food and to the young ravens which cry. He delighteth not in the strength of the horse, He taketh not pleasure in the legs of a man. The Lord taketh pleasure in them that fear Him, in those that hope in His mercy.

Then shall be said the *Lord's Prayer* and the following:

We thank Thee, Lord God, Heavenly Father, through Jesus Christ our Lord, for all Thy benefits; who livest and reignest for ever and ever. Amen.

---

[1] All get enough to eat. Care and avarice alike prevent satisfaction.

LUTHER'S SMALL CATECHISM.

TABLE[1] OF DUTIES; OR, CERTAIN PASSAGES OF SCRIPTURE FOR VARIOUS HOLY ORDERS AND ESTATES, WHEREBY THESE ARE SEVERALLY TO BE ADMONISHED OF THEIR OFFICE AND DUTY.

To Bishops,[2] Pastors, and Preachers.

A bishop must be blameless, the husband of one wife, vigilant, sober, of good behaviour, given to hospitality, apt to teach; not given to wine, no striker, not greedy of filthy lucre; but patient, not a brawler, not covetous; one that ruleth well his own house, having his children in subjection with all gravity; not a novice.[3] Holding fast the faithful Word as he hath been taught, that he may be able by sound doctrine both to exhort and convince the gainsayers. 1 Tim. iii. 2, 3, 4, 6; Tit. i. 9.

What the Hearers Owe to Their Pastors.

Eat and drink such things as they give; for the laborer is worthy of his hire. Luke x. 7.

Even so hath the Lord ordained that they which preach the Gospel should live of the Gospel. 1 Cor. ix. 14.

Let him that is taught in the Word communicate unto him that teacheth in all good things. Be not deceived; God is not mocked; for whatsoever a man soweth, that shall he also reap. Gal. vi. 6, 7.

Let the elders that rule well be counted worthy of double honor, especially they who labor in the Word and doctrine. For the Scripture saith, Thou shalt not muzzle the ox that treadeth out the corn; and the laborer is worthy of his reward. 1 Tim. v. 17, 18.

---

[1] To be hung up to be observed by every one in the house.
[2] In the New Testament an overseer of the congregation, *i. e.*, a Pastor. Afterwards, also overseer of several pastors and congregations.
[3] One who has just begun to believe.

TABLE OF DUTIES.

And we beseech you, brethren, to know them which labor among you, and are over you, in the Lord, and to esteem them very highly in love for their work's sake. And be at peace among yourselves. 1 Thess. v. 12, 13.

Obey them that have the rule over you, and submit yourselves; for they watch for your souls, as they that must give account; that they may do it with joy, and not with grief: for that is unprofitable for you. Heb. xiii. 17.

Of Civil Government.

Let every soul be subject unto the higher powers. For there is no power but of God: the powers that be are ordained of God. Whosoever therefore resisteth the power, resisteth the ordinance of God; and they that resist shall receive to themselves damnation. For rulers are not a terror to good works, but to the evil. Wilt thou then not be afraid of the power? do that which is good, and thou shalt have praise of the same: for he is the minister of God to thee for good. But if thou do that which is evil, be afraid; for he beareth not the sword in vain: for he is the minister of God, a revenger to execute wrath upon him that doeth evil. Rom. xiii. 1-4.

Of Subjects.

Render unto Cæsar the things which are Cæsar's; and unto God the things that are God's. Matt. xxii. 21.

Wherefore ye must needs be subject, not only for wrath, but also for conscience sake. For, for this cause pay ye tribute also; for they are God's ministers, attending continually upon this very thing. Render therefore to all their dues: tribute, to whom tribute is due; custom, to whom custom; fear, to whom fear; honor, to whom honor. Rom. xiii. 5-7.

I exhort therefore, that, first of all, supplications, prayers, intercessions, and giving of thanks be made for all men; for kings, and for all that are in authority; that we may lead a quiet and peaceable life in all godliness and honesty. For this is good and acceptable in the sight of God our Saviour. 1 Tim. ii. 1–3.

Put them in mind to be subject to principalities and powers, to obey magistrates, to be ready to every good work. Tit. iii. 1.

Submit yourselves to every ordinance of man for the Lord's sake: whether it be to the king, as supreme; or unto governors, as unto them that are sent by him for the punishment of evil-doers, and for the praise for them that do well. 1 Pet. ii. 13, 14.

To Husbands.

Likewise, ye husbands, dwell with them according to knowledge, giving honor unto the wife, as unto the weaker vessel, and as being heirs together of the grace of life; that your prayers be not hindered. And be not bitter against them. 1 Pet. iii. 7; Col. iii. 19.

To Wives.

Wives, submit yourselves unto your own husbands, as unto the Lord. Eph. v. 22.

Even as Sarah obeyed Abraham, calling him lord; whose daughters ye are as long as ye do well, and are not afraid with any amazement. 1 Pet. iii. 5, 6.

To Parents.

And, ye fathers, provoke not your children to wrath: but bring them up in the nurture and admonition of the Lord. Eph. vi. 4.

To Children.

Children, obey your parents in the Lord: for this is right. Honor thy father and mother; which is the first commandment with promise: that it may be well with thee, and thou mayest live long on the earth. Eph. vi. 1–3.

TABLE OF DUTIES.

To Servants, Hired Men, and Laborers.

Servants, be obedient to them that are your masters according to the flesh, with fear and trembling, in singleness of your heart, as unto Christ; not with eyeservice, as men-pleasers; but as the servants of Christ, doing the will of God from the heart; with good will doing service, as to the Lord, and not to men: knowing that whatsoever good thing any man doeth, the same shall he receive of the Lord, whether he be bond or free. Eph. vi. 5–8.

To Masters and Mistresses.

And, ye masters, do the same things unto them, forbearing threatening; knowing that your master also is in heaven; neither is there respect of persons with Him. Eph. vi. 9.

To the Young in General.

Likewise, ye younger, submit yourselves unto the elder. Yea, all of you be subject one to another, and be clothed with humility: for God resisteth the proud, and giveth grace to the humble. Humble yourselves, therefore, under the mighty hand of God, that He may exalt you in due time. 1 Pet. v. 5, 6.

To Widows.

Now she that is a widow indeed, and desolate, trusteth in God, and continueth in supplication and prayers night and day. But she that liveth in pleasure, is dead while she liveth. 1 Tim. v. 5, 6.

To all in Common.

Thou shalt love thy neighbor as thyself. Herein are comprehended all the commandments. Rom. xiii. 9. And persevere in prayer for all men. 1 Tim. ii. 1.

> Let each his lesson learn with care,
> And all the household well shall fare.

Lord, open Thou my heart to hear,
And by Thy Word to me draw near,
Let me Thy Word still pure retain,
Let me Thy child and heir remain.

Thy Word doth move the inmost heart,
Thy Word doth perfect health impart,
Thy Word my soul with joy doth bless,
Thy Word brings peace and happiness.

Glory to God, the Father, Son,
And Holy Spirit, Three in One!
To Thee, O blessed Trinity,
Be praise throughout Eternity!
John Olearius, 1671.

INTRODUCTORY QUESTIONS.*

1. What little book have you in your hand?

The Small Catechism of Dr. Martin Luther.

2. What is the meaning of Catechism?

Instruction.

3. What instruction does this book give?

It tells that which I must know that I may be saved.

4. Who prepared this book?

Dr. Martin Luther.

5. Who was he?

He was a famous Doctor of the Church of God, a teacher of Theology at Wittenberg, in Saxony.

6. When did he live?

More than 300 years ago. He was born November 10, 1483, at Eisleben, and died there February 18, 1546.

---

*It will be well for the teacher, at the beginning of every lesson, to go over it with the child, then to let him read over the Questions and Answers with him, and finally to question him freely, letting him look on the book meanwhile,—and so to proceed until the child knows what he ought to know.

7. You call this Luther's Small Catechism: did he prepare more than one?

Yes; in the same year he prepared a Large Catechism, too.

8. In what year was that?

1529.

9. Did Dr. Luther tell his own wisdom in his two Catechisms?

No. He put together in brief and told the wisdom of God, as it is revealed to us in the Holy Scriptures.

10. What then is Luther's Small Catechism?

It is a summary of God's wisdom, or of the Word of God.

11. Is it so regarded?

Yes. It has been given a place among the Confessions of Faith of the Lutheran Church, and for more than three hundred years has been a favorite book of the Church.

12. What name did Dr. Luther give to his Small Catechism?

Enchiridion or Handbook.

13. Why did he so name it?

Because the young were always to have it in, and at, hand, and to learn it.

14. What does it contain?

a. A remarkable Preface, addressed to all faithful and pious Pastors, which tells how the Catechism is to be taught and learned.

b. The six Parts of the Catechism.

INTRODUCTORY.

c. How a Father may teach his household to pray, morning and evening.

d. The Table of Duties for all estates of men.

15. What is the most important part of the Catechism?

The Six Parts.

16. And what are they?

The *first* treats of the *Holy Ten Commandments.*

The *second*, of the *Holy Christian Faith.*

The *third*, of the *Holy Lord's Prayer.*

The *fourth*, of the *Sacrament of Holy Baptism.*

The *fifth*, of the *Sacrament of the Altar.*

The *sixth*,* of the *Office of the Keys* and *Confession.*

---

* This is called the *Sixth Part*, though put in the *fifth* place, because it was added after all the rest.

INTRODUCTORY QUESTIONS TO THE FIRST PART.

II.

17. What is the subject of the First Part?

The Holy Ten Commandments.

18. What one word means the same thing?

The Law.

19. What is the Law?

That which God has ordained to be the rule of all that we do, or leave undone,—God's will in reference to us.

20. How can a man learn what the Law is?

From his conscience, and from the revelation of God.

21. What knowledge of the Law does a man derive from his conscience?

It is not clear, and it is imperfect. Yet it is there. Even the heathen "shew the work of the law written in their hearts, their conscience also bearing witness, and their thoughts the meanwhile accusing, or else excusing one another." Rom. ii. 15.

QUESTIONS TO FIRST PART. 41

22. And what knowledge of the Law do we get from Revelation?

It is pure and clear. There is shown "what is good, and what the Lord doth require of thee." Micah vi. 8.

23. Where do we find the revelation of the will of God?

In the Ten Commandments, of which we have been speaking.

24. Who gave the Ten Commandments?

The Lord God Himself. Ex. xx.; xxxi. 18; xxxii.; xxxiv. 1, 28, 29. Deut. v. 10ff.

25. To whom did He give them?

To His people Israel.

26. Are they not in force for the Church of the New Testament also?

Certainly. Christ, the Mediator of the New Testament, says, "Think not that I am come to destroy the Law or the Prophets: I am not come to destroy, but to fulfil. For verily I say unto you, Till heaven and earth pass, one jot or one tittle shall in no wise pass from the Law till all be fulfilled. Whosoever therefore shall break one of these least commandments, and shall teach men so, he shall be called the least in the kingdom of heaven; but whosoever shall do and teach them, the same shall be called great in the kingdom of heaven." Matt. v. 17–19.

27. Where did God give these Commandments?

In the wilderness, at Mt. Sinai.

28. Where are the Wilderness and Mt. Sinai?

In Arabia, a peninsula of Asia.

29. When did God give this Law?

On the fiftieth day after the exodus of the children of Israel from Egypt.

30. What name is given to the day of the Exodus?

The Passover. (Easter.)

31. And to the fiftieth day after?

Pentecost, which is the Greek word for *fifty* (Whitsunday).

32. Did God Himself say these Commandments from the mountain?

"These words the Lord spake unto all your assembly in the mount out of the midst of the fire, of the cloud, and of the thick darkness, with a great voice." Deut. v. 22. And all the people heard them. Ex. xx. 18ff.

33. What did the people do, when they heard and saw this?

They fled and were sore afraid.

34. Why then did the Lord speak so terribly?

That we might dread His anger, and not do anything against His Commandments. Ex. xx. 5.

35. Were not the Commandments of God written, for the people and their descendants?

Yes. The Lord Himself wrote them on two tables of stone and gave them to Moses. Ex. xxxii. 16.

QUESTIONS TO FIRST PART.

36. And what do the Scriptures call these two tables?

"The two tables of testimony, tables of stone, written with the finger of God." Ex. xxxi. 18.

37. To whom did God give these two tables of testimony?

To His servant, Moses the prophet, who had led the children of Israel out of Egypt to Mt. Sinai. Deut. v. 22.

38. What did Moses do with the tables of testimony?

He threw them out of his hand and broke them at the foot of the mountain. Ex. xxxii. 19.

39. Why did he do this?

Out of fierce anger, because when he came down to the camp he saw that forty days after God had given them the Law, the children of Israel were carrying on their idolatry again with a golden calf. Ex. xxxii.

40. Did not God punish Moses for breaking the tables?

No, not at all. Ex. xxxiv. 1; Deut. iv. 13, x. 1, 2.

41. But what did Moses have to do?

Hew out two tables for himself and come with them up into the mountain. Ex. xxxiv. 1; Deut. x. 1.

42. And what did the Lord do?

"He wrote on the tables, according to the first writing, the Ten Commandments, and gave them to Moses." Deut. x. 4.

43. What may be the meaning of the two tables of the Law?

The human heart, in which the commandments of God ought to be written.

44. What may be the meaning of the first tables, which God Himself made?

The human heart, as it was created by God.

45. And of the tables which Moses made?

The human heart, as it was made by man through his fall.

46. What is to be found on both pairs of tables?

God's own writing, the Ten Commandments.

47. And what is the meaning of this?

That one and the same holy will of God had been revealed both before and after the fall, in Paradise and on Sinai.

QUESTIONS ON
THE MEANING OF THE WORDS OF THE FIRST PART.

III.
Introduction to the Commandments.

48. What did God say and write at the beginning of the First and of all the Commandments?

Just as earthly princes set their names before their decrees, that it may be known from whom the decrees come, and who is offended if the decrees are not obeyed, so the Lord put His Name before His Commandments, that every man may know that he keeps or breaks the commandments of so great a God.

49. What is the beginning of God's Commandments?

I am the LORD thy God. Ex. xx. 2; Deut. v. 6.

50. What is the Hebrew of the word LORD?

Jehovah. Ex. iii. 14.

51. What is the meaning of Jehovah?

I AM THAT I AM.

52. What all is expressed by this word?

The meaning of this name is deeper than the sea: it cannot be found out. Yet we see clearly,

He is *Eternal;*

He is *Unchangeable*, without variableness, faithful to Himself in word and deed;

An Eternal, Unchangeable, Truthful, Faithful, Inscrutable Being.

First Commandment.

53. What does the First Commandment forbid?

To have other gods.

54. What does that mean?

To worship other gods.

55. Since you should not worship other gods, whom should you worship?

Him who says, I am the LORD thy God.

56. Are there other gods?

"Beside Him there is no God." Is. xliv. 6, xlv. 5; Deut. vi. 4.

57. And according to the explanation of this Commandment what shall you do?

Fear, love and trust in God.

58. And how much shall you fear, love and trust in Him?

Above all things.

59. What does that mean?

More than all things.

60. And why should you fear, love and trust in, Him above all things?

Because nothing is so great, so dear, and so faithful, as the LORD my God.

61. And what are you doing if you fear, love and trust in anything more than God?

I am putting a creature into God's place.

62. And what are you making of this creature?

My idol.—From this may the LORD my God preserve me. Amen.

IV.

Second Commandment.

63. What is forbidden in the Second Commandment?

To take the Name of the LORD our God in vain.*

64. What is the Name of the LORD our God?

The LORD, or Jehovah.† Ex. iii. 14.

65. Has not God other names also?

Yes. He has many names, but He calls Himself Jehovah and keeps this name for Himself alone.

---

* From the earliest time there have been two ways of dividing the Ten Commandments given in Ex. xx. 1-17. While some have joined verses 4, 5, to the First Commandment, others have made a Second Commandment out of them, of our Second a Third, and so on, and have made our Ninth and Tenth into one. The *Reformed* have accepted this division, while the *Lutherans* have kept the former division, for which more can be said.

† In order not to take the Name of Jehovah in vain, and really to keep the Second Commandment, the Jews did not utter it at all, but whenever it occurs in the Old Testament they read instead of it *Adonai*, which means *Lord*. Consequently we no longer know whether the word ought to be pronounced *Jehovah*, or in some other way. Therefore, after the example of the Jews, all our versions of the Scriptures have the Word LORD, where the word Jehovah is found in the Hebrew. In an English Bible, whenever the word stands for the Hebrew Name *Jehovah*, it is printed in small capitals, LORD.

48 LUTHER'S SMALL CATECHISM.

66. May you take any of the names of God in vain?

I may misuse none of the names which belong to God, or by means of which I think of Him.

What is it "to take in vain"?

67. How, according to the explanation in the Catechism, is the Name of God taken in vain?

By cursing, swearing, using witchcraft, lying or deceiving.

What is it to curse? to swear? to use witchcraft? to lie? to deceive?

68. What does the LORD say of those who take His Name in vain?

The LORD will not hold him guiltless that taketh His Name in vain. Ex. xx. 7.

69. For what purpose is the Name of the Lord given to us, according to the explanation in the Catechism?

That we may call upon, worship, praise and thank Him. Therefore for all kinds of prayer.

What is the meaning of calling upon Him? Worship? Praise? Thanksgiving?*

70. What should keep us from taking God's Name in vain, and what should urge us to the right use of it?

The fear and love of God, out of which flows the observance of all the Commandments.

---

*Nothing is easier than to teach to call on God, pray, praise and thank Him. Of *Calling on God*, see Luther's *Large Catechism* at the end of the Second Commandment. (*Müller's* edition, p. 399f, §§ 70–77). As to *Prayer*, let the teacher keep to his definitions. "What is it to pray? What have you to ask of God?" Here let him tell the needs of our souls and bodies. "How do you speak to your father, when you ask him for something to eat?" Answer: "Dear father, I pray you give me some bread." "Well. Speak in the same way to your heavenly Father, with this difference only, that in His presence, which you always are in, you should speak with adoration and perfect confidence."—In the same way *praise* and *thanksgiving* may be

THE COMMANDMENTS.

71. How does Dr. Luther begin the explanation of every Commandment, because the observance of all the Commandments flows from the fear and love of God, or from the observance of the First Commandment?

He begins the explanation of every commandment by repeating the explanation of the First: *We should fear and love God, and &c.*

72. Is all cursing and swearing forbidden?

No.

73. Is all witchcraft, lying and deceiving, forbidden?

Yes, all.

74. Why is not all cursing forbidden?

Because (Deut. xxvii. 15–26) God bade all the people say *Amen* to His curse.

---

explained. "What is it to praise? Tell me what God is like, and what He has done?"—Here teach simply and with practical examples the sweet doctrine of the Attributes of God, which a child will need only a little 'encouragement to find *via negationis et eminentiæ*. When the attributes (Names) of God have been recounted, then say a *Sursum Corda* (not in Latin, of course not in an unknown tongue), and tell the child to name the attributes and works of God in the presence of God. E. g. "Merciful and gracious is the Lord, longsuffering, etc." Or, "Thou hast made me. Thou hast preserved me. Thou art the Creator of all things. Thou upholdest all things." The Hallelujah Psalms afford an excellent example, and a child will understand them.—And so with *Thanksgiving*. "What is it to give thanks?" Answer: "To recognize and own that a thing is God's gift." "Tell me some of God's good gifts." "What do you say when you give thanks?" "That I live, that I see the light, that I hear Thy voice, etc., all is Thy good gift, given to me though I do not deserve it. I know this, and I own it before Thee and Thy angels and all the world. For this I thank Thee."—Many Psalms will show how praise and thanksgiving are woven together. The same deed of God can be regarded as mark of His greatness and of His kindness; the same Attribute (Name of God) will show His glory and His kindness to us. Proof: "We thank Thee for Thy great glory;" His Word is His glory and our Salvation.—The author knows by experience how easy and short and yet how instructive such training of the children in prayer is. Only, to avoid levity, such exercise should not be too frequent. To many children it is sweet and blessed.

50   LUTHER'S SMALL CATECHISM.

Because our Lord Jesus cursed. Matt. xi. 21, xxiii. 13–16, 23–29; Mark xi. 13, 21.

75. Why is not all swearing forbidden?

Because God, Gen. xxii. 16; Ps. cx. 4; Christ, Matt. xxvi. 63, 64, v. 18ff.; Heb. vi. 13, 14; the angels, Dan. xii. 7; Rev. x. 6; and holy men of God, Gen. xiv. 21, 22; 1 Sam. xx.; 2 Cor. i. 23, have sworn; and, besides, the word of the Old Testament cannot be broken, which says, Thou shalt fear the LORD thy God, and serve Him, and shalt swear by His Name. Deut. vi. 13, x. 20.

76. But is not all swearing forbidden in Matt. v. 34, 37, and James v. 12?

It is impossible that God should contradict Himself. Christ did not come to destroy the Law, but to fulfil it (Matt. v. 17.) The oath, which was commanded in the Old Testament, and used in both the Old Testament and the New by God and angels and men, cannot be rejected by Christ and His Apostles.

77. What sort of swearing is forbidden in those passages?

Not that which is commanded in the Old Testament, but the misuse by the Jews (Matt. xxiii. 16), who in daily life swore wantonly and by creatures, when they might have said simply *Yes* and *No*, or in a case of necessity might have sworn by the Name of God.

78. What cursing and swearing is forbidden therefore in the Second Commandment?

Not that which uses the Name of God, but

THE COMMANDMENTS.

that which without reason and wickedly misuses it.

79. Is all witchcraft, lying and deceit forbidden in the Second Commandment?

All witchcraft, lying and deceit are forbidden, but not in the Second Commandment; but only the witchcraft, lying and deceit which misuse the Name of God.

V.
Third Commandment.

80. What is bidden in the Third Commandment?

To remember the Sabbath day to keep it holy.

What is meant by the Sabbath day? What is it, to keep holy?

81. Which day of the week was the holy day of the Old Testament?

The seventh, or Saturday.

82. Why was the seventh day kept in the Old Testament?

God blessed the seventh day and hallowed it, because on it God rested from all the works which He had made. Gen. ii. 2, 3; Ex. xx. 8–11. The seventh day was a memorial of completed creation.

83. What is the holy day of the New Testament?

The first day of the week, Sunday.

84. Why do we no longer celebrate the old Sabbath?

Because through St. Paul the Lord says to the Colossians (ii. 16): "Let no man judge you concerning holy days and new moons and Sabbaths." Gal. iv. 10.

85. But does not this break the Law of the Old Covenant, of which in Matt. v. 17-19 the Lord says, that it cannot be broken?

No, for the Lord Himself, who is the Lord of the Sabbath (Mark ii. 27, 28), did not break the holy day of olden time, but fulfilled its meaning (Heb. iv.), and brought in the new time, which no longer counts from the rest-day of creation.

86. Is another day commanded in the New Testament, instead of the seventh day?

No. No such commandment, either of the Lord, or of His Apostles, has come down to us.

87. Why then has a special holy day been fixed?

One day must be set on which the people may know that they are to come together to hear God's Word and to cherish the communion of believers by means of the Word and the Sacrament.

88. Was the Church free to choose any day of the week?

Yes, since we were not to be judged concerning any day.

89. Why then was not the seventh day chosen?

Just because the Jews held that God made it necessary to observe the seventh day. Christian freedom from the Old Testament Sabbath Law is asserted.*

---

*See the *Augsburg Confession*, Art. xxviii. "For they that think that the observation of the Lord's day was appointed by the authority of the Church, instead of the Sabbath, as necessary, are greatly deceived. The Scripture, which teacheth that all the Mosaical ceremonies can be omitted after the Gospel is revealed, has abrogated the Sabbath. And yet, because it was requisite to appoint a certain day, that the people might know when they

THE COMMANDMENTS.

90. And why was the first day chosen?

Because the Lord Himself had hallowed it by His resurrection from the dead and the outpouring of the Holy Ghost, as in the Old Testament He hallowed the seventh day by resting from the Creation. The best and holiest recollections of Christian men are connected with this day.

91. And why do we still keep this day?

Although chosen in Christian freedom, it has

---

ought to come together, it appears that the [Christian] Church did for that purpose appoint the Lord's day: which for this cause also seemed to have been pleasing, that men might have an example of Christian liberty, and might know that the observation, neither of the Sabbath, nor of any other day, was of necessity."

Also *Large Catechism:* "We keep the festal days, not for the sake of intelligent and learned Christians (for they have no need of this observance), but first of all for bodily causes and necessities, which nature teaches and requires; and for the common people, man-servants and maid-servants, who are occupied the whole week with their work and trade, that for a day they may forbear, in order to rest and be refreshed. Secondly, and most especially, that on such a day of rest, time and opportunity be taken to attend divine service, and afterward to praise God in singing and prayer. * * * In itself no one day is better than another, and this should indeed occur daily; but since the mass of people cannot give such attendance, there must be at least one day in the week set apart. * * Since from of old Sunday has been appointed for this purpose, we should also continue the same, that everything be done in order. * * * The day needs no sanctification for itself. * * God desires it to be holy to thee. Therefore it becomes holy or unholy on thy account, according as thou art occupied on the same with things that are holy or unholy. How then does such sanctification occur? Not that with folded hands we sit behind the stove and do no rough work, or deck ourselves with a garland and put on our best clothes, but that we occupy ourselves with God's Word and exercise ourselves therein. * * * * Since, then, so much depends upon God's Word that without it no Sabbath can be kept holy, we ought to know that God will insist upon a strict observance of this Commandment, and will punish all who despise His Word, and are not willing to hear and learn it, especially at the times appointed for the purpose."

been from the beginning the favorite day of Christian people, and a mark of the New Covenant, just as the old Sabbath was a mark of the Old Covenant; it is, moreover, an outward sign of the inner unity between Christians, of the communion of saints, of those who have fallen asleep who kept it, and of those who are living on the earth.

92. But may you not for yourself make a work-day of Sunday?

By so doing I not only would reject the day, but would withdraw myself from the Word of God and from the Communion of Saints.

93. Do we then cling to this day?

Yes; but not for the day's sake, but for the sake of the Word and of the Communion, which from of old belong to this day, from which we withdraw if we do not keep this day.

94. Have we reason, then, to accept the word of the Lord, Remember the Sabbath day to keep it holy?

Yes, indeed. The day on which the greatest events of the New Testament took place, and which the Church has always chosen for its publication of the Word and for its Communion, can be despised by individual persons only to the injury of their own souls.

95. What is the important matter in reference to the New Testament Sabbath?

Not the day, but that by which all days and all things are sanctified, the Word of God and prayer. 1 Tim. iv. 5.

THE COMMANDMENTS.

96. What is the explanation of the Third Commandment?

We should fear and love God, and not despise preaching and His Word, but keep it holy and gladly hear and learn it.

97. Are preaching and the Word of God the same thing?

No. A pious man's sermon reflects God's Word, like a mirror reflects the light of the sun; but in comparison with the Word of God the sermon always is imperfect. The Word always is a perfect revelation of divine saving wisdom and truth.

98. How should we receive the Word of God which we hear on Sunday?

We should keep it holy.

What does this mean?

99. Is it enough to "keep it holy"?

We must diligently and gladly hear it.

100. Is it enough to hear it?

We must also learn it, that faith may come by hearing. For faith cometh by hearing. Rom. x. 17.

VI.

Fourth Commandment.

101. What does the Lord command in the Fourth Commandment?

He commands me to honor my father and my mother.

What is it to honor?

102. Whom besides parents does the explanation include in the Fourth Commandment?

Masters.

103. Who are our "masters"?

All who are placed over us, "whether it be the king as supreme, or governors as those sent by him," (1 Peter ii. 13–15, 18) and also masters and housefathers. And those also who are at the head of churches and congregations may also be included. 1 Tim. v. 17. 1 Thess. v. 12, 13. Heb. xiii. 17. And also teachers.

104. Why have all these a place in the Fourth Commandment?

Because all who are set over us, are in our parents' place, and therefore the Scriptures call them fathers.*

105. What does the explanation say you must not do if you would honor your parents?

Neither despise them nor provoke them to anger.

106. And what does it say a child ought to do to its parents in order to honor them?

Honor, serve, obey, love and esteem them.

Define these words.

107. How has the Lord especially distinguished this Commandment?

It is the first commandment with promise. Eph. vi. 2, 3; for He says, Ex. xx. 12, Honor thy father and thy mother, that thy days may be long in the land which the Lord thy God giveth thee.

---

* "All whom we call masters are in the place of parents and must derive their power and authority to govern from them. Hence also they are all called fathers in the Scriptures."—Luther in the *Large Catechism*. Read there the whole glorious explanation of the Fourth Commandment.

THE COMMANDMENTS.

108. But do not many pious children die young?

These do not receive a temporal promise, but in the world to come they receive far more exceedingly according to the fullness of promises which He has given for eternity.

109. But what are you to do if your parents or masters are bad, do all kinds of wickedness, and unreasonably burden their children and others subject to them?

Even then they are my parents or masters, whom I must honor, serve, obey, love and esteem.

110. But what if they require of you what is against God's Word and the honor due to Him, and against their salvation and your brother's?

Yet I will honor them, serve them, love and esteem them, but I will not obey them when they command what is contrary to God's Word and the honor due to Him and to my salvation and my brother's.

111. And why?

We must obey God rather than men, Acts v. 29; iv. 19. And God will not have us resist the Holy Ghost "as our fathers did." Acts vii. 51.

VII.

Fifth Commandment.

112. What does the Fifth Commandment forbid?

To kill.

113. What else according to the explanation is also forbidden?

To hurt or harm our neighbor in his body.

114. To whom shall we do no harm?

Our neighbor.

115. And what shall we not hurt?

Our neighbor's body.

116. How is such an explanation drawn from the Commandment?

The greatest injury to a man's body is death; and this cannot be done if we do no harm or injury to our neighbor's body.

117. Which is greater, hurt or harm?

Harm.

118. What is the beginning of any hurt or harm we may knowingly and willingly do to our neighbor?

It begins in our souls, in hatred, envy, unkindness; therefore Christ (Matt. v. 21 ff.) stopped the source of murder, when He forbade and threatened to punish anger.

119. Who is our neighbor?

He whom we are nearest to, with whom we associate, who needs us, even if he be a Jew, or our enemy.

120. Are we forbidden to hurt or harm the body of our neighbor only?

It is forbidden to do ourselves such injury.

121. If we are forbidden to hurt or harm our neighbor in his body, is it wrong for a father to chastise his child?

No, for the Lord Himself says (Prov. xxiii. 13, 14, *cf*. xiii. 24), Withhold not correction from the child; for if thou beatest him with the rod, he shall not die. Thou shalt beat him with the rod, and deliver his soul from hell.

THE COMMANDMENTS.

122. But is it not a sin if the courts order a murderer to be put to death, or that some other bodily punishment be visited on a godless person?

No. God says (Gen. ix. 6), Whoso sheds man's blood, by man shall his blood be shed. And in the Garden of Gethsemane our Lord said (Matt. xxvi. 52), Whosoever taketh the sword shall perish by the sword; and Paul writes to the Romans (xiii. 4), The power is a minister of God to thee for good. But if thou do that which is evil, be afraid; for he beareth not the sword in vain; for he is the minister of God, a revenger to execute wrath upon him that doeth evil.

123. But is it not wrong for soldiers to kill in battle?

Not only in the Old Testament, but in the New, there are warriors who were well-pleasing to God. And when the soldiers asked John Baptist, What shall we do? he said, Do violence to no man, neither accuse any falsely; and be content with your wages (Luke iii. 14). He did not say they must give up their place and calling.

124. And what is our duty, according to the explanation?

To help and befriend.

What do these words mean?

125. In what should we help and befriend?

In every bodily need.

126. Give me instances of such bodily need?

Poverty, sickness, nakedness.

127. Is there in the New Testament a special arrangement for the exercise of this duty?

Yes, the office of *deacons* (Acts vi. 1-6), which continued for a long time in the Church, although now it is wanting in many congregations.

128. If we are to help and befriend our neighbour in every bodily need, in what case should we do still more for him if we can?

In every need of his soul.

VIII.

The Sixth Commandment.

129. What is here forbidden?

To commit adultery.

130. What is marriage?

It is the public and lasting union of a man and a woman in the closest fellowship of body and life.

"A man shall leave his father and mother and cleave unto his wife, and they twain shall be one flesh," Gen. ii. 24. "So they are not twain, but one flesh." Matt. xix. 5, 6.

131. Who instituted marriage?

God Himself in Paradise. God made woman out of a rib He took from a man, and brought her to him. Gen. ii. 22. Male and female did He make them. And He blessed them. Gen. i. 27, 28.

THE COMMANDMENTS. 61

132. Why did God institute marriage?

That man might not be alone, but might have a help meet for him, and that they might multiply upon the earth. Gen. ii. 18; i. 28.

133. And what further purpose came in after the Fall?

On account of fornication (*i. e.* for the avoidance of fornication), let every man have his own wife, and every woman her own husband. 1 Cor. vii. 2.

134. How has the Lord glorified earthly marriage?

By making it a figure of the highest and eternal marriage, the marriage between Christ and His Church. Ez. xvi. 8 f.; Eph. v. 32.

135. What do man and wife promise each other at the very beginning of marriage?

That they will love one another, as Christ loves His Church, and the Church loves Him. Eph. v. 22–33; Gen. ii. 18, 24.

136. And how does Christ love His Church?

Perfectly,—so that He gave up heaven and earth, to seek her and cleave to her.

Exclusively,—One, says He, is my dove. Cant. vi. 8.

Unchangeably,—I will betroth myself to thee forever. Hos. ii. 19.

Holily, and *unto Sanctification*,—"He gave Himself for the Church, that He might sanctify and cleanse it by the washing of water by the Word, that He might present it to Himself a glorious Church, not having spot, or wrinkle, or any such thing; but that it should be holy and without blemish." Eph. v. 25-27.

137. And how does the Church love Him?

Perfectly, exclusively, indissolubly, as He loves it, for it is in His school, and is subject to Him (Eph. v. 23) and fears Him (Eph. v. 33).

138. How then ought Christian husbands and wives love each other?

Perfectly, exclusively and indissolubly, holily and unto sanctification; and the wife should obey and fear her husband.

139. What is the difference between the human marriage of man and wife and the marriage of Christ with His Church?

That is for a season; when one of the parties dies, the marriage is at an end (1 Cor. vii. 39): this is eternal. So far as Christ is concerned, it is perfect; but the marriages of men and women are imperfect.

140. How is a human marriage broken?

When one is loved not exclusively, or not unchangeably; when the heart thinks of or seeks another or gives itself to another; or when the precious bond is broken by adultery; or one forsakes the other.

141. Does Christ allow no divorce, no dissolution of the marriage tie?

No. Only when marriage is broken, whether by fornication (Matt. xix. 9), or by wicked desertion, in the case mentioned by St. Paul (1 Cor. vii. 15), the innocent party is free.

THE COMMANDMENTS. 63

142. What leads to adultery in most cases?

An unchaste heart and disorderly company.

Who is chaste? Who is pure?

143. To what therefore does the Explanation of the Sixth Commandment especially exhort husbands and wives?

To be chaste and temperate in words and deeds.

144. But are only those who are married to be chaste and temperate?

No, the single too.

145. Are maiden and wifely chastity one and the same thing?

No. Chastity in those who are married, cleaves to husband or wife alone; but maiden chastity is free from every man or woman.

146. Which is better?

They are of like worth (1 Cor. vii.). Those who forbid to marry, teach a doctrine of devils (1 Tim. iv. 1–3).

147. Which is easier?

It depends on the person. If one have the gift of continence, it is easier to live unmarried.

148. Is it possible to live chastely in either of these states?

Yes, by the grace of God, though our sinful nature and evil imagination often resists His grace.

149. What is a great help to the chastity of the married, and generally in the married life?

That one not only love, but honor, his wife or her husband.

150. And why is so much stress laid on honoring?

Because when respect dies, love ceases. Respect daily nourishes love. Marriage without love and honor never can prosper.

IX.

The Seventh Commandment.

151. What is forbidden in the Seventh Commandment?

To steal.

152. What is it, to steal?

To take secretly and wrongly.

153. What does the Explanation say we are not to take or steal?

Our neighbor's money or property.

154. How can our neighbor's money or property be taken from him?

Secretly or by open violence.

155. What is it called, when our neighbor's property is taken secretly?

Theft, or stealing.

156. What, when it is taken by open violence?

Robbery.

157. The Explanation mentions another way of taking our neighbor's money or property. What is it?

By false wares or dealing.

158. What name is given to this sort of stealing?

Cheating.

159. How can a man steal by means of "false wares?"

When a man gives bad wares instead of

good, or, in general, gives other things than those he promised.

160. And how, by "false dealing?"

By false wares, false weights, false measures, counterfeit money, usury, extortion, "taking advantage by expert arts and uncommon transactions or dexterous inventions, in short by getting the best of the bargain and wantonly oppressing and distressing" our neighbor. See the *Large Catechism*.

161. What shall he do who has broken this Commandment?

Eph. iv. 28: "Let him that stole, steal no more: but rather let him labour, working with his hands the thing which is good, that he may have to give to him that needeth." 2 Tim. ii. 19: "Let every one that nameth the name of Christ depart from iniquity."

162. And what shall be done with what he had stolen?

Ex. xxii. 3. He should make full restitution. Ez. xxxiii. 15. "If the wicked restore the pledge, give again that he had robbed, walk in the statutes of life, without committing iniquity; he shall surely live, he shall not die." Compare also the working of God's grace on Zacchæus, Luke xix. 8.

163. But if he refuse to do this?

Then he neither repents nor believes. He has not God's forgiveness, and God's threat against thieves hangs over him. 1 Cor. vi. 10.

164. What ought we do, according to the Explanation of the Seventh Commandment?

Help our neighbor to improve and protect his property and living.

165. Why is not our neighbor's money mentioned here, as in the first part of the Explanation?

Because it belongs to his property.

166. Why is our neighbor's living mentioned specially?

Because his property depends on his living, i. e., on what he earns. This living is the source of his money and property.

167. Why is it said we should help him to improve and protect it?

Because we cannot improve and protect it ourselves; we can only help him to do so; our neighbor and others must help too; and especially does he need the Helper of all helpers, Almighty God.

X.

The Eighth Commandment.

168. What is forbidden in the Eighth Commandment?

To bear false witness against our neighbor.

169. What is witness?

Every opinion, every utterance, which we form or express concerning anything, is a witness.

170. What witness is called false?

First, that in which heart and word are false; and secondly, that in which the words are right, but heart and purpose are false.

THE COMMANDMENTS.

171. Is only false witness before a court of law forbidden in this Commandment?

Though we should least of all give false testimony in court, yet this Commandment forbids all false witness.

172. What does the Explanation of the Eighth Commandment reckon to be false witness?

Four things: *falsely to belie* our neighbor, i. e., to lie about him;
betray him;
slander him;
defame him.

Define these words.

173. In how many of these cases are both heart and word false?

In three—lying, slander and defamation.

174. In which of them may the words be right, while the heart is false?

Betrayal.

175. What is it to betray any one?

To tell his secrets to his harm.

176. How can the words be right in such a case?

Because the secret may be told as it is.

177. But why is the heart false?

Because the secret is told to hurt our neighbor.

178. What, for instance, was the truth told by Judas?

The secret resort of Jesus.

179. And why do you say Judas' heart was false in this?

Because he intended to hand over his Master into the hands of His enemies.

180. It is wrong to give false witness against our neighbor; would it be allowable to bear false witness for him?

No. Neither the heart nor the word of a Christian man may depart from the truth, whether the issue be for or against our neighbor. Deut. xvi. 20; Lev. xix. 15; Ps. xxxiv. 13.

181. Is it right to give true witness against our neighbor?

Certainly, and we must do it when necessary.

182. But this might do him harm?

It is not best to shrink from hurting a sinner, if the hurt may be wholesome for his soul. It often serves to rescue innocence, and the welfare of many or of all, and the honor of the Lord, to say the truth of a man to his hurt.

183. But is it not generally thought to be betrayal, if one speak truth to the injury of his neighbor?

But it is not so. We should do right, that truth may be honored in word and deed.

184. What more must we do, according to the Explanation of the Eighth Commandment?

Excuse our neighbor, speak well of him, and make the best of all he does.

What is it to excuse? When ought we speak well of any one? What do you mean, by making the best of all he does?

185. Ought we in all cases, excuse our neighbor, speak well of him, and make the best of all he does?

No, for then we would often have to pervert the truth. We cannot deny proven guilt, we cannot call evil good, open baseness we cannot call right, without bearing false witness.

186. What shall we do, when in any particular case we are in doubt whether to excuse, speak well of, or make the best of, anything?

Let love decide, which walks without blame in the kingdom of truth (Eph. iv. 15), which is long-suffering and kind, and believes, hopes and bears all things (1 Cor. xiii. 4, 7), and is an enemy of all falsehood.

XI.

The Ninth Commandment.

187. What is forbidden in the Ninth Commandment?

To covet.

188. What does it forbid us to covet?

Our neighbor's house.

189. To what is this extended in the Explanation?

His inheritance or home.

190. If we are forbidden to wish for our neighbor's inheritance or home, is it wrong to wish to buy an inheritance or house?

To wish to buy anything is not forbidden. It is not an unrighteous wish if the desire ceases as soon as the sale is refused.

191. But what, then, does the Ninth Commandment forbid?

Two things: to craftily seek to gain our neighbor's inheritance or home, and to get it by a show of right.

192. And why is this forbidden in the Explanation?

Because it is the bad fruit of a bad, unrighteous desire for our neighbor's inheritance or home.

193. What desire for a neighbor's inheritance or home do you call unrighteous?

That which does not regard the inviolability of another's property, but aims at getting it without and against the will of its just owner, which may be done craftily or with an appearance of legality.

194. What does the Explanation bid us do?

To help and serve our neighbor.

195. In what?

In keeping his inheritance or home.

Tenth Commandment.

196. What is forbidden in this Commandment?

Coveting, again.

197. And what are we here forbidden to covet?

Anything that is our neighbor's.

198. What is mentioned especially?

His wife, manservant, maidservant, and cattle.

199. What, according to the Explanation, are we forbidden to do to our neighbor's cattle?

Let them loose, or drive them away.

200. How?

Without our neighbor's knowledge and consent.

201. What are we not to do to his wife and servants?

Estrange them, or entice them away.

202. But what, on the other hand, ought we do?

Urge them to stay and do their duty.

XII.

Of the Ninth and Tenth Commandments.

203. What is then forbidden in the Ninth Commandment?

All lust or coveting.

204. And in the Tenth?

Coveting, again.

205. Lusting after what, is forbidden in the Ninth Commandment?

After one thing, our neighbor's house.

206. And what lust is forbidden in the Tenth?

After anything denied to me and given to another; all sorts of desires of what others have.*

207. What do you call the evil disposition of the soul which sets all its desire on one thing which it is forbidden to have?

A passion. In the Ninth Commandment, as it is given Ex. xx. 17, the passion of avarice is forbidden.

208. What name does the Church give to "passion?"

Actual lust.

209. Why is it so called?

Because it urges, and does not rest, till evil is done.

---

*Ex. xx. 17, the Ninth Commandment forbids to covet our neighbor's *house*; and the Tenth, to covet his *wife*. But in Deut. v. 21, in the repetition of the Commandments, the *wife* is mentioned in the Ninth, and the *house* in the Tenth. This shows that the distinction of the two Commandments does not depend on the distinction between *house* and *wife*, but that in the Ninth, a coveting of one thing, and in the Tenth, all coveting of all sorts of forbidden things, is censured.

210. What, therefore, is forbidden in the Ninth Commandment?

Lust.

211. And what is the miserable disposition called, which, dissatisfied with what itself has, grudges a neighbor whatever he has, his wife, his household, his cattle, in short whatever he may have?

Covetousness and discontent.

212. Who is free from such a disposition?

Naturally, no one. Only Christ the Lord.

213. And whence have we this discontented and covetous heart?

It is handed down from parents to children, ever since the Fall of Adam.

214. And what do you call it therefore?

Inherited lust. (Natural Concupiscence.)

215. Which Commandment opposes to inherited lust all the authority of the Lord?

The Tenth,—in forbidding all the wandering desire of the soul, all wishing for what is our neighbor's.

216. Is natural concupiscence the same thing as "original sin?"

No. It is only a part of it.

217. What is original sin?

Inherited and inborn lust and inclination to evil—and also inherited and inborn powerlessness in respect of what is right.

218. By what is evil lust awakened in man?

The Commandment. St. Paul, in Rom. vii. 7, 8, says, "I had not known sin but by the

THE COMMANDMENTS.   73

Law: for I had not known lust, except the Law had said, Thou shalt not covet. But sin, taking occasion by the Commandment, wrought in me all manner of concupiscence; for without the Law sin was dead."

219. What is the result of the excitement of inborn lust?

Actual lust, with all actual sin in word and deed.

220. And how does actual lust come out of the sinful desire in our hearts?

When a man takes pleasure in sinful desire and yields his will to its temptation. "Every man is tempted, when he is drawn away of his own lust, and enticed. Then when lust hath conceived, it bringeth forth sin; and sin, when it is finished, bringeth forth death." James i. 14, 15.

221. What does the Tenth Commandment show us?

The source of all actual sin.

222. And what is the source of all good works?

Fear, love and trust in God, *i. e.* the fulfilment of the First Commandment, to which I am admonished by the explanation of every other Commandment.

223 And how does this become the source of all truly good works?

The fear of the Lord is the beginning of wisdom. Love is the fulfilling of the Law. And they that trust in Him bring forth fruit without ceasing. We will neither do wrong, nor

74   LUTHER'S SMALL CATECHISM.

neglect what is right, if we live in observance of the First Commandment.

224. What, however, resists the observance of the First Commandment?

Inborn powerlessness and disinclination to good. Original sin, which tempts me to all evil, hinders all my attempts to do right.

XIII.

The Conclusion to the Commandments.

225. What does the Lord thy God call Himself?

A jealous God.

226. Who is "jealous?"

One who is strict in requiring the love due him.

227. If God is strict to require the love due to Him, what does He find?

He finds that men rather hate, than love Him;

That fathers bring up their children to hate Him;

And that the children walk in the footsteps of their parents. 1 Pet. i. 18.

228. Are there really men who hate God, and who bring up their children to hate Him?

St. John says (1 John v. 3), "This is the love of God, that we keep His Commandments." And therefore a persistent disobedience to His Commandments can be nothing but a hatred of God.

THE COMMANDMENTS.

229. If now, the Lord sees generation after generation walk in hatred to Him, what does He do?

He visits the sins of the fathers upon the children, *i. e.*, He punishes the children with their fathers and like their fathers, because with and like their fathers they walk in hatred to Him.

230. And what is His purpose in so doing?

That He may bring the children from the way of their fathers.

231. And how far does He continue to do so?

To the third and fourth generation.

What is a generation?

232. Will He then avenge the sins of parents on pious children?

No, He speaks of fathers and children that *hate Him.* If children do not follow the sin of their parents they will not follow them in the punishment. Jer. xxxi. 29. Ez. xviii. 2.

233. But what if it does no good to visit the iniquities of the fathers upon the children to the third and fourth generation?

Then He will destroy the children of such parents on account of their obstinate hatred and disobedience, as is to be seen in the case of the kings of Israel.

234 But what does He promise to them that love Him and keep His Commandments?

He will show mercy unto thousands of them. Ex. xx. 6.

235. What, according to the Explanation, is contained in these words concerning the Commandments?

Threatening and promise. He threatens to punish all who transgress these Commandments. He promises grace and every blessing to all who keep them.

236. Why does He threaten us?

That we may fear His wrath and not break His Commandments.

237. And why does He give a promise?

That we may love and trust in Him, and gladly do what He has commanded us.

QUESTIONS LEADING TO PART II.

XIV.

238. Have you dreaded God's displeasure, and not transgressed His Commandments? Have you loved and trusted Him and gladly done what He has commanded?

Alas, No. I often have broken all the Commandments of my God, in my thoughts, my words and my deeds; oftener than I can tell; and therefore I have deserved God's wrath and punishment.

239. Will you henceforth keep God's Commandments better than in the past?

I am not able to. "I know that in me, that is, in my flesh, dwelleth no good thing." Rom. vii. 18.

240. And have you then no hope of amendment?

Yes, I have. "God works in us, both to will and to do of His good pleasure." Phil. ii. 13.

241. But are you not already lost because of your countless transgressions?

No. "Christ has redeemed us from the curse of the Law, being made a curse for us." Gal. iii. 13.

242. How do you know that you are freed from the curse of the Law, and that God will make you better?

From the *Gospel*.

243. And how will God make you better?

Through the Gospel, given by the Holy Ghost to them that hear. Gal. iii. 2.

244. Will you then ever be perfectly clean and holy before you die?

No. Sin, which clings to me even until death, will not let me be perfect. Even to the day of my death I will find sin and weakness in the best things I do.

245. Where do you learn the Gospel?

In Part II. of the Catechism, to which we are coming now.

246. Is the First Part of the Catechism useless to you because you neither could keep the Law of the Lord, nor can now keep it as you ought to?*

Certainly not. It has been of use to me hitherto as a bar and a looking-glass, and I hope it will also prove to me a bit and bridle.

247. How has it been a "bar" to you?

Just as a wild beast when caged still is a wild beast, but the bars will not let him break out and do harm, so the Law keeps an unconverted man from giving rein to all the bad impulses that are in him.

---

*For this reason all of us, to the day of our death, must pray the Fifth Petition: "Forgive us our trespasses, as we forgive those who trespass against us." No one can do more than St. Paul, Rom. vii. 14ff. Though in our Baptism we are washed all over, we need the daily washing of our feet by our Lord, for our feet in their daily walk daily become dusty, and new sin cleaves to our souls every day. John xiii. 10.

248. And in what sense is it a looking-glass?

I see in the Law the sinfulness of my soul. "Through the Law is the knowledge of sin." Rom. iii. 20.

249. And how can it be a bit and bridle?

Just as a well-broken horse can be guided by a gentle motion of the hand, and even of a finger, so a man who has been renewed by God's Word, and has a good will, can be led and guided by the law of God on the way to eternal life. Matt. xi. 30.

250. And what do you need above all else, in order that the Law may become this to you, and that you may learn and keep this third use of it?

That I learn the Gospel from this Second Part of the Catechism, and from the Gospel receive the Spirit, who will renew and confirm my spirit in obedience to God's Commandments.

QUESTIONS
INTRODUCTORY TO PART II.

XV.

251. What do you call the Second Part of the Catechism?

The Creed.

252. What is the meaning of that word?

It means 1. a statement of what we ought to believe, and 2. the belief of our hearts.

253. What is a Creed?

A Confession of Faith, which may be written or printed, or may merely be kept in the memory.

254. And what do you mean by the "Belief of the heart?"

The certain assurance that all divine saving truth is what the Confession of Faith or Creed contains and confesses.

255. But is not faith, according to Heb. ii. 1, the substance of things hoped for, the evidence of things not seen?

Yes. But the Creed tells what things are hoped for, and what are the things not seen.

256. By which faith are we saved, the Creed or the belief of the heart?

By neither alone, but by both together. He who does not know what to believe is saved as little as he who does not believe what he ought.

QUESTIONS TO SECOND PART. 81

The Creed without faith helps not at all; and faith is impossible without a Creed.

Remark.—Just as head, memory, mouth and heart belong to one and the same man, so creed and faith, confession and assurance, belong together and are one.

257. Where do you find a statement of what you ought to believe in your heart?

In the Apostles' Creed.

258. Why do you call it " the Apostles' Creed ?"

Because it precisely agrees with the words and teachings of the Apostles.

259. Are there other Creeds?

The Nicene, of the year 325, the *Athanasian* (of the former part of the fifth century), the *Augsburg Confession* and its *Apology* of 1530, the *Smalkald Articles* of 1537, and the *Formula of Concord* of 1579. The *Small* and the *Large Catechisms* are also confessions of the Church.

260. What is the difference between these Confessions?

They do not contain different beliefs, but they belong to different periods, have different ends, and exhibit different manners of composition. One explains and completes the other, but all agree in the same faith.

261. Does the whole Second Part of the Catechism belong to the Apostles' Creed?

No. The Explanation, though quite worthy of the text, comes not from the Apostles, nor from their time, but from Dr. Martin Luther.

262. How is the Apostles' Creed divided?

Into three Articles.

263. What does the first Article of Faith confess?

The First Person of the Godhead, the Father, and His works.

264. And what are His works?

Creation and Providence.

265. And what does the Second Article confess?

The Second Person of the Godhead, the Son, and His work—Redemption.

266. And what does the Third Article confess?

The Third Person of the Godhead, the Holy Ghost, and His work—the sanctification of mankind in His holy Church.

267. And is our Creed therefore a lovely picture of the Holy Trinity?

Yes. As there is one true eternal God and in Him three Persons; so have we one faith, but in that one Faith are there three Articles.

OF THE HOLY TRINITY.

XVI.

The doctrine of the Holy Trinity is not expressly treated in Luther's Small Catechism, but it is presupposed, for a man is to grow in belief of it from the hour of his birth. The proof of the doctrine easily may be drawn from the Holy Scriptures, thus:

It is without doubt that the Lord is One God. Ex. xx. 3; Deut. vi. 4; Mark xii. 29; 1 Cor. viii. 6; Is. xliv. 6, 8.

Just as little question can there be, that the Holy Scriptures ascribe the names of God, His Attributes, Works and Glory, to three Persons.

1. To the *Father*. E. g. Eph. i. 3, 7.
2. To the *Son*. John i. 1, 3, 5, 22, 23; ii. 25; viii. 58; xvii. 5; xxi. 17; xx. 28; xii. 41, compared with Is. vi. 1; Acts xx. 28; Rom. ix. 5; Col. i. 16, 17: 1 Tim. iii. 16; Heb. i. 3, 6; Rev. i. 8; Jer. xxiii. 6; Micah v. 1; Is. xl. 3.
3. To the *Holy Ghost*. Acts v. 3, 4, 9; 1 Cor. ii. 10, 12; iii. 16; xii. 4-6, 11; Heb. ix. 14.

We find all three together. Matt. iii. 13ff; xxviii. 19; 2 Cor. xiii. 13.

If there is One Divine Being, yet three distinct Divine Persons, these Three Persons must be One Divine Being, and this One Divine Being must be in each of these Three Persons. This is a secure conclusion of faith. The doctrine is far beyond our understanding; but thus has God revealed Himself, thus will He be worshipped, so is He.

This knowledge of the Triune God is necessary to eternal life, because eternal life consists in the true knowledge of God, John xvii. 3. No one has the Father who has not the Son and the Spirit, 1 John ii. 23, Rom. viii. 9, and no one can receive the Baptism that saves, except in belief and confession of the Triune God. Matt. xxviii. 19.

QUESTIONS ON
THE MEANING OF PART II.

XVII.

268. What is the subject of the First Article?
Creation.

What is the meaning of Create? Creator? Creation?

269. To which of the three Persons of the Godhead is creation especially attributed?
To the First, the Father.

270. On whom do you therefore believe in the First Article?
God the Father.

271. Why do you call Him Father?
In distinction from the Second Person of the Godhead, the Onlybegotten Son, Who is in the bosom of the Father (John i. 14, 18), Whom we confess in the Second Article.

272. What is the Father?
The Creator.

273. And what did He create?
Heaven and earth.

274. What is the word for heaven and earth together?
The World, or the Universe.

275. What do you call God because He was able to make heaven and earth?
The Almighty.

276. What, according to the Explanation, do you believe?
That God has made me.

277. You only?
No. Together with all creatures.

What is "a creature?"

278. Where do you find a description of Creation?
In the first two chapters of the Bible.

279. In how many days did God make heaven and earth?
In six days.

280. What did He make on the first day?
Heaven and earth, and day and night.

281. And what were the works of the other days?
On the second, God finished the heavens;
On the third, sea and land, and all plants;
On the fourth, sun, moon and stars;
On the fifth, fishes and birds;
On the sixth, land animals and man.

282. Which are the noblest of God's creatures?
Angels and man.

283. What are the angels?
Glorious spirits, without bodies such as we have. Heb. i. 7; Col. i. 16.

284. Were they created before the world?
No. God ended all His work in six days.

Gen. ii. 1, 2. Ps. civ. 3, the Angels are reckoned among the works of God.

285. When were they made?

We do not know, though Ps. civ. 3 may include them on the second day.

286. What is the difference between men and angels?

Man is a spirit, but he has also a body of flesh and bone.

287. Where do you find an account of the creation of man?

In the first, but especially in the second, chapter of the Bible.

288. What did God give to man at his creation?

Body and soul.

289. And what did He give to the body?

Eyes, ears and all its members.

290. Why does the Catechism mention eyes and ears particularly?

Because these are at the present our principal members, and the most useful to our eternal salvation.

291. What use do you make of your eyes?

With them I see God's glory in His works —and read the Bible.

292. And of your ears?

With them I hear His works, especially His saving Word.

293. What did God give to your soul?

Reason and all my senses.

294. What use do you make of reason?

By it my spirit grasps what God's Spirit says to me in His Word.

295. What do you understand by "all your senses?"

The other powers of the soul, such as the will, the memory, &c.

XVIII.

296. Did the angels remain in their first estate?

Not all. Many abode not in the truth (John viii. 44), but sinned (2 Pet. ii. 4): kept not their high estate but forsook their habitation (Jude vi.).

297. When did that take place?

After Creation had been finished; for when He had finished all, God said that it was good. Gen. i. 31.

298. How many kinds of angels are there, since then?

Two, *good* and *bad*.

299. Where did evil begin?

In the angels, some of whom turned their mind and will away from God.

300. Have men continued to be what God made them?

No. Misled by the devil, the prince of the fallen angels, Eve, and then Adam, fell. Gen. iii.

301. And what was the consequence of the fall?

Adam and his posterity became bad. Gen. v. 3; vi. 3, 5; viii. 21.

302. What did Adam thereby lose?

The likeness of God in which he had been created; which before the fall he possessed in his completeness, freedom, immortality and strength of body and soul; and which now he will have to put on again. Gen. i. 16–28; Col. iii. 10; Eph. iv. 24.

303. Has God now turned away from men altogether?

No. Although they became miserable and continually fell more and more into forgetfulness of God and into sin, He resolved to redeem them, and promised One who should bruise the serpent's head, Gen. iii. 15, and conquer hell.

304. Have the holy angels forsaken sinful men?

No, for their Creator has not. They are all ministering spirits, sent forth to minister to them that shall be heirs of salvation. Heb. i. 14.

305. And what does the Lord in His mercy still do for men?

Preserves us.

306. How does the Catechism express this?

He *still* preserves me.

307. What is implied by the word "still"?

It is an admiring hint of the depth of our fall and of the unfathomableness of God's grace.

308 Does the Lord give and preserve to us only our bodies and souls and all our senses?

No. Besides, He gives and preserves many things, without which I could not exist.

THE CREED.

309. What does He give to cover the poor body of fallen man?
Clothing and shoes. Gen. iii. 21.

310. What for its nourishment?
Meat and drink.

311. What for shelter?
House and home.

312. What for affection and society?
Wife and child.

313. What for work and employment?
Land, cattle and goods.*

314. And how do you say He gives you all?
He provides me with all that I need for this body and life.

What is *Need?*

315. Why does the Catechism say, "Of this body and life"?
Because we are speaking here of temporal benefits only, and have not yet come to the redemption of men from all evil, and the glory of the promised body and life.

316. And in what measure does He provide?
Richly.

317. And how long and how often?
Daily.

318. And is that the end of His goodness?
No. He protects me.

---

*See how good God is to poor fallen man, and owns him as His creature. Of what use is clothing without food—or food without shelter—or this without affection and society—and even this, if he have not occupation?

What is it "to protect?"

319. Against what does He protect you?

Against all danger.

320. And what more does He do?

He keeps and guards me.

What do these words mean?

321. From what?

All evil.

322. The First Article is said to treat of Creation and Providence: How then does care, protection, preservation and guarding come into it?

God provided for us 1. by supplying all our wants, and 2. by protecting, keeping and guarding us against all evil.*

323. Why does God do all this?

Purely out of fatherly divine goodness and mercy.

324. And without what on your part?

Without any merit or worthiness in me.†

325. And what do you therefore owe God?

For all this I am in duty bound to thank and praise, to serve and obey Him.

Here examine yourself.

326. How do you confirm what you have just confessed?

This is most certainly true.

---

*Give to a child everything it needs; care for it as you may; if you protect it not from wind and weather, from murderers, thieves and wild beasts, against sickness and infirmities, how long will it live?

†All this God does to His enemies also. Therefore we speak of His *universal love*.

THE CREED.

327. What old word of another tongue expresses this?
Amen.

XIX.

328. On whom do you believe in the Second Article?
In Jesus Christ.

What is the meaning of the name "Jesus"?
What is the meaning of "Christ"?

329. Who is Jesus Christ?
The Son of God.

330. Are you not a son and child of God?
Yes, but not in the same sense in which Jesus is God's Son.

331. Why not?
I am an adopted child of God, and so are all other believers on earth. Christ, however, is born of God's own substance, God of God. No one else can say this of himself.

332. What does the Creed therefore call Jesus Christ, in contradistinction from all other sons?
The Only-begotten Son of God. John i. 14, 18; Col. i. 15.

333. Of whom did His mother conceive Him?
Of the Holy Ghost.* Luke i. 26–38.

334. Of whom was He born?
Of the Virgin Mary.† Luke ii. 1–20.

---

* At Nazareth in Galilee.—*Feast of the Annunciation*, March 25.
† At Bethlehem, in Judea—CHRISTMAS, December 25.

335. Why is she called the Virgin?

Because she is the promised Virgin beyond compare, and because before and after the birth of her blessed Son she remained a Virgin. Is. vii. 14.

336. Was this wonderful Son of God and of the Virgin received by the world as He deserved to be?

No. He was not treated as He ought to have been. "He came unto His own, and His own received Him not." John i. 11.

337. What happened to Him?

After thirty-three years of weary life came the heavy Passion, of which the Creed says, *He suffered.** Matt. xxvi. 27; Mark xiv. 15; Luke xxii. 23; John xviii. 19.

338. Under whom did He suffer?

Under Pontius Pilate, the governor appointed by the Roman Emperor. Matt. xxvii. 11ff.; Mark xv. 1ff.

339. What shameful punishment was inflicted?

He was crucified, Matt. xxvii. 31–35; Mark xv. 25ff.; Luke xxiii. 33ff.; John xix. 16–25.

340. And what was the awful end of this?

He died.† Matt. xxvii. 50; Mark xv. 37; Luke xxiii. 46; John xix. 30.

341. Do we certainly know that He did die?

Yes, we know it by the testimony of God

---

* In and near Jerusalem—the *Passion*, from ASH WEDNESDAY to the GREAT SABBATH.

† At Jerusalem, on Mt. Calvary, Golgotha—on GOOD FRIDAY.

THE CREED.

and men. It had been foretold by the holy Prophets (Is. liii.) "Thus it behooved Christ to suffer, and be preached to all nations." Luke xxiv. 46, 47. On the Cross our Lord Himself commended His spirit into His Father's hands, Luke xxiii. 46, and then gave up the ghost. Many saw and heard it, (Luke xxiii. 47-49). The soldiers pierced His side with a spear-wound, into which a man might put his hand. John xix. 33f; xx. 27. And Pilate also inquired carefully concerning His death. Mark xviii. 44, 45.

342. And what occurred after His death?

He was buried in the new tomb of the counsellor Joseph of Arimathea.* Matt. xxvii. 60; Mark xv. 42-46; Luke xxiii. 50-53; John xix. 38-42.

Remark.—The whole life of our Lord, from His lowly birth in the stable at Bethlehem to His death and burial, is called the state of His *Humiliation*.

343. Did He remain dead and in the grave?

Not at all. "He had power to lay down His life, and He had power to take it again." John x. 18. He had this power and He proved it.

344. How, in the first instance?

He resumed His life in the body on Easter Morning and descended into Hell. Eph. iv. 8-10; Col. ii. 15; I Pet. iii. 18-20.

---

* From Good Friday night until Easter morning He lay in the tomb of Joseph of Arimathea—THE GREAT SABBATH.

345. And what was the object of His descent into Hell?

That upon the strong man armed the Stronger than he might come (Luke xi. 21), to solemnly take from the devil unto Himself the power of death (Heb. ii. 14), and also to fill Hell with the glory of His Divine-human Person (Eph. iv. 8ff.), to triumph over the powers of Hell openly (Cor. ii. 15), and to show to the lost the righteousness of faith in its victory and triumph, which they had despised and mocked (1 Pet. iii. 18ff.).

346. What followed the descent into Hell?

He rose again from the dead.* Matt. xxviii. 6ff.; Mark xvi. 6; Luke xxvi. 5-7; John xx.

347. And when was this?

On Easter Morning, on the third day after His death.

348. Did He show Himself to His own after His resurrection from the dead?

Yes. The women saw Him, then Mary Magdalene, then Cephas (Peter), the two on the way to Emmaus, the Ten—all on Easter; eight days afterwards, the Eleven saw Him; the disciples saw Him, at the Sea of Tiberias; on the mountain in Galilee He was seen by above five hundred brethren at once; then by James; and finally, by all the Apostles at His Ascension. 1 Cor. xv. 1ff. John xxi.

---

*EASTER—since the Council of Nicaea, celebrated on the Sunday after the full moon that follows the 21st of March.

THE CREED.

349. Why did He appear to them so often?

To render His disciples certain that He had risen, and to talk with them of the kingdom of God. Acts i. 3; Luke xxiv. 25ff. ; 44ff.

350. What occurred on the fortieth day after Easter?

He ascended into Heaven.* Mark xvi. 19; Luke xxvi. 50, 51; Acts i. 9–11.

351. Why did He thus go up to Heaven?

"That He might fill all things." Eph. iv. 10.

352. And where is He since His ascension?

He sitteth at the Right Hand of God the Father Almighty.

353. Are we to understand by this merely that He sits in the body on the throne of glory?

No. To sit at the Right Hand of God means to be equal with God in power and glory. Matt. xxviii. 18.

354. Is He now far away from us who are on the earth?

In virtue of His entrance upon the Father's power and glory He can fulfil His promise, "Behold, I am with you alway, even unto the end of the world," Matt. xxviii. 20; and "Wheresoever two or three are gathered in my Name, there am I in the midst of them." Matt. xviii. 20.

---

* At Bethany, on the Mount of Olives, on the fortieth day after Easter—which always falls on a Thursday—ASCENSION DAY.

355. Will He always remain hidden from us in His great glory, or will He come again?

From thence also He will come again. Matt. xxiv. 30. Now He fills heaven and earth with His divine-human glory, without our seeing it. But He will come visibly, as He went visibly. Acts i. 10, 11.

356. And for what purpose will He come?

To judge the quick and the dead. Matt. xxv. 31.

What is it, "to judge?" Who are "the quick?"

Remark.—The life of our Lord, from the Descent into Hell, is called the state of *Exaltation*. His humiliation did not last long, but His exaltation has no end, but endures from everlasting to everlasting.

XX.

357. What, according to the Explanation of the Second Article of the Creed, do you believe about Jesus Christ?

That He is my Lord.

358. And what does the Explanation call Him?

True God. 1 John v. 20.

359. Of whom is the Son, True God, begotten?

Of the Father.

360. And when was He begotten of the Father?

From eternity.

361. Which is greater, the Father or the Son?

"As is the Father, such is the Son, and such is the Holy Ghost." (See the Athanasian Creed.) Each Person of the Godhead is equal to the other, in essence and power and glory.

THE CREED.

362. But what else does the Explanation call our Lord?

True man.

363. How can you prove that He was True Man?

Because He had a human soul, which could both rejoice and be troubled even unto death (Luke x. 21; Matt. xxvi. 38), which in dying He committed into the hands of His Father, which was separated from the body; and a human body, which was born, lived, suffered and died, as our bodies do.

364. Of whom was the true Man Jesus Christ born, according to the explanation?

Of the Virgin Mary.

365. What difference is there between God the Father, God the Son, and God the Holy Ghost?

God the Son is also true man; but the Father, like the Spirit, is only true God. The Son became man for our sake, but the Father and the Spirit did not.

366. How many natures therefore are united in the Second Person of the Trinity, since He became Man?

Two: the divine nature and the human nature are truly united in one person in Christ.

XXI.

367. Is Christ now according to His Divine-human Person equal to the Father?

Equal to the Father according to His Godhead, less than the Father according to His humanity. (Athanasian Creed.) John x. 29, 30; xiv. 28.

368. There is no one like the Son of God. Holy and glorious is His Name, and highly exalted above every name. What, however, were you, from your youth up?

A lost and condemned creature.

369. What is a lost creature?

One who always goes wrong, who never can find the end of his being and the way to it, who has no hope of coming to his eternal home.

370. What is a condemned creature?

One on whom God's curse lies and shuts him out from his eternal home and from salvation.

371. And why were you a lost and condemned creature?

I was lost, because I did not know the way to eternal life; I was condemned, because God had laid His curse upon me and had delivered me to death and the devil.

372. You were lost and condemned: are you not still?

No. The Lord Jesus, the great Son of God and of the Virgin, has taken my soul to His heart, that it might not perish.

373. And how has He done this?

He has redeemed, purchased and won me.

What is the meaning of redeemed? of purchased? of won?

374. What has He redeemed, purchased and won you from?

From all sins, on account of which I was condemned, and in which I went astray.

375. And from what else?

From death* and from the power of the devil, †to which I was given over.

376. In how far has He delivered you from sins?

He bore the curse of sin for me, He broke the dominion of sin over me, and in Him I am free from sin and its control.

377. In how far has He purchased you from death?

His death has broken the sting of my death, and my flesh shall rest in hope, for He has brought life and immortality to light by His resurrection.

378. And in how far has He won you from the devil?

He has taken away the devil's power over me, freed me from the kingdom of darkness, and translated me into the kingdom of love and light.

379. Wherewith did He redeem, purchase and win you?

Not with silver and gold.

380. Why?

Gold and silver could not redeem immortal souls from the bondage of sin, from the chains of death, and from the power of the devil.

---

*"Death is the wages of sin"—he who sins, falls into bodily and spiritual, temporal and eternal death. Through Christ we are freed from all death, even from the death of the body. For our flesh also rests in hope, and that our souls are delivered from this body of death, is a blessing.

†The sinner is under the power of the devil by his own fault and by the righteous sentence of God. But Christ reconciled us to God, satisfied His righteousness, and won for Himself a right to us.

381. But wherewith did our Lord Jesus Christ redeem you?

With His holy precious blood, and with His innocent sufferings and death.

382. And why did He have to give His body and life for your redemption and that of all poor sinners?

The rule is, *soul for soul*. That I might not be given over to the devil, on account of my sin, and to death, He, my substitute, had to innocently die for me, becoming my lamb of sacrifice. "Without shedding of blood there is no remission of sins." Heb. ix. 22. Therefore St. John Baptist pointed to Him, and with him we sing, O Christ, thou Lamb of God, that takest away the sins of the world, have mercy upon us! Grant us Thy peace! Is. liii.; John i. 29.

383. Inasmuch as He has bought you with such a price, what is your confession?

He redeemed me that I might be His.

384. If He then has acquired a perfect right to you, so that He is your Lord and you belong to Him, what follows?

That I am in my Lord's power, body and soul, for time and for eternity, and His will must be mine.

385. And what is His will concerning you, since you are His?

That I should live under Him in His kingdom and not in the world, as before, nor under the prince of this world, the devil.

386. And what do you mean by living under Him?

To live according to His will, to serve Him.

THE CREED.

387. And what does the word "live" mean here?

Never to die, to live forever.

388. And why do we live in His kingdom forever?

His kingdom is an everlasting kingdom; He is an everlasting King, who gives eternal life to His people.

389. What does the Catechism therefore say of this life under Him?

That we may serve Him in everlasting righteousness, innocence and blessedness.*

390. Can you not attain to this everlasting righteousness, innocence and blessedness until after death, in the kingdom of Heaven?

His kingdom is here now, and I receive everlasting righteousness, innocence and blessedness now, as soon as I come into His kingdom through repentance and faith.

391. But do you not sin every day?

But He is righteous, and His righteousness is mine, and in it even the righteousness of my own life is made to grow.

392. But how can you be innocent in all your guilt?

I am innocent through the forgiveness of my sins.

393. And are you not saved?

Yes, I am saved, though in hope only. My sadness lessens daily, and daily my joy becomes more complete.

---

* Here see the Son in His glory, and on His neck the redeemed soul in eternal beauty! Beautiful as is the end of the Explanation of the First Article, the close of the Explanation of this Article is yet more glorious. This draws us to the Lord. What a God! Where is a God who comes so near to His people?

394. But how can you speak of everlasting righteousness, innocence and blessedness? Will you not die?

All will be with me as it was with Christ; like as He is risen from the dead, lives and reigns to all eternity.

395. What does this mean?

Just as through death Christ came to His eternal throne, instead of being shut therefrom, so my body and my soul will not be deprived of eternal life through death. I will rise from the dead, and with Him live and reign to all eternity.

396. And what do you, with the Explanation, say to this?

Amen. This is most certainly true.

XXII.

397. On whom do you believe in the Third Article?

The Holy Ghost.

398. Who is the Holy Ghost?

The Third Person of the Godhead, equal to the Father and the Son in essence, majesty and glory.

399. What do you believe concerning the Holy Ghost?

That from all eternity He proceeds from the Father and from the Son, and has been sent by the Father and by the Son for the sanctification of men.

400. What is the meaning of the words, "He proceedeth from the Father and the Son?"

They denote the manner of the origin of the

THE CREED.

Third Person of the Trinity, as it is described in the Athanasian Creed:

"The Father is made of none: neither created, nor begotten.

"The Son is of the Father alone: not made, nor created, but begotten.

"The Holy Ghost is of the Father, and of the Son: neither made, nor created, nor begotten, but proceeding."

All our imagination and thought fall short of this thrice-holy mystery.

401. Is all Christendom agreed in the doctrine of the procession of the Holy Ghost from the Father and the Son?

No. The Eastern church believes that the Holy Ghost proceeds from the Father alone.

402. Why?

Because no express word declaring His procession from the Son is found in the Scriptures.

403. Why then is it believed in the West?

Because otherwise the Father and the Son would not be equal. John xvi. 15.

Because otherwise the order of Persons would not be clear, nor would it be evident which is the Second, and which the Third Person.

Because otherwise the Holy Ghost would be sent by the Father alone, and not by the Father and the Son. John xv. 26; xvi. 7; xiv. 26.

Because otherwise the Spirit could not be called the Spirit of the Son. Gal. iv. 6.

404. What more do you believe in the Third Article?

The Church.

405. What is the Church?

The communion of saints.

406. Why is it called the communion of saints?

Because all the saints of God are collected in it or belong to it.

407. Whom do you call "saints?"

According to Holy Scripture, not only the perfected saints of God in heaven, but also the saints who are becoming holy on earth, those called to be saints, who not yet are what they are to be, and what they can become and will become. Rom. i. 7; 1 Cor. i. 2; Eph. i. 1.

408. Are there not then two Churches and communions of saints, one of the called, and one of the perfect?

No. We believe only one Church, to which all the saints of all ages and all places belong in time and eternity.

409. And what name do you give to the one Church, because all saints of God belong to it here and in the world to come?

One holy Church.

410. But are not unholy men mixed with the Church here on earth?

Yes. As tares were sown among the wheat, so are there hypocrites and lip-worshippers in the Church. Still, the Church gets its name from the holy in it, as the field remained a wheatfield in spite of the tares; and her true members seek daily purification in the forgive-

THE CREED.

ness of their sins, and through daily brotherly love and pastoral care, and through Christian discipline (Matt. xviii. 15ff.) aim at the sanctification of the whole as well as of the several parts.

411. What further name is given to the Church in the Creed?

Christian.

412. Why is the Church called "Christian?"

She bears the name of Christ her Head, whose body she is—and who is her foundation, on which she is built up a spiritual habitation and temple of God. Eph. iv. 15f.; 1 Cor. iii. 11.

413. Why do we say, "I believe the holy Church," and not, in the holy Church?

Because we believe "in" the three Persons of the Holy Trinity.

414. Why is the Church mentioned in the Third Article, which refers to the Holy Ghost?

When the Holy Ghost was poured out on Pentecost, He founded the Church. It is born of Him through the Word and Sacraments, it is His work, and at the same time His workplace and instrument for the salvation of mankind.

415. Where is the Church?

Where God's Word and Sacraments are. Matt. xxviii. 19.

416. Who belong to it?

All who believe and are baptized. Mark xvi. 16; Acts ii. 40-42.

417. But are there not many different Churches?

Alas, yes, through human guilt, which will not obey the truth, many parties have arisen in the Church; but in comparison with the rest only one is true.

418. And which is the true Church?

That which teaches and confesses God's Word purely, and administers the Sacraments according to the institution of Christ. John viii. 31; x. 27.

419. What Church does this?

The so-called Lutheran church, to which therefore the titles Christian and Apostolic belong especially.

420. How can you find out what the Lutheran Church teaches?

From her confessions, which no Lutheran preacher dare contradict.

421. What are those Confessions?

The three General Creeds, the Augsburg Confession and the Apology, the Schmalkald Articles, the two Catechisms of Luther, and the Formula of Concord. They are all printed together in the Book of Concord, published in 1580.

422. How do we know that these Confessions accord with the Holy Scriptures?

By comparing them with the Holy Scriptures.

423. And how can you find out how the Lutheran Church administers the Sacraments?

From the Liturgies, which no pastor dare disregard.

THE CREED. 107

424. But how can you know that the Liturgies agree with the institution of Christ?

By comparing them with it.

425. Can any one be saved in other Churches?

Yes, because they possess more or less of the saving treasure of the Word and Sacraments of God.

426. Would it be right to remain in another Church then?

No, not after discovering its errors. One would not dare remain knowingly in a church, after he recognized that its teachings are false and its sacraments are wrongly administered, for to do so would make him a partaker in the guilt of false doctrine and practice.

427. Is it right to receive the communion in a Church which teaches falsely or administers the sacraments falsely?

Inasmuch as we become one body, one church, with those with whom we eat the one bread, yet ought not become one with an heretical communion, 2 John 11, we cannot commune with any church from which we have separated, or which has separated from us, on account of the truth. 1 Tim. vi. 3-5; Tit. iii. 10.

428. What then is the proper behaviour towards other, i. e. false Churches?

Not to partake of the communion at their altars, but to testify against their errors by word and deed; but not to deny that their members are saved, leaving that to Him who judgeth righteously.

XXIII.

429. What else do you believe in the Third Article?

The forgiveness of sins.

430. Why is the forgiveness of sins mentioned immediately after the Church?

Because the forgiveness of sins is the great Gospel through which the Church is gathered and preserved unto that day.

Remark. The forgiveness of sins is treated in the II., III., IV., V., VI. Parts, because it is the subject of the whole Catechism.

431. Why is it found in the Third Article?

Because it is the word and comfort of the Spirit and His best gift.

432. What else do you believe in the Third Article?

The resurrection of the body.

433. Is it possible that any one will rise from the dead?

Yes, for Christ has risen.

434. But is it possible for the body to rise, after it has decayed?

Christ did not see corruption, but we shall see corruption. The body can rise again, for Lazarus rose again, and the corruptible bodies of the saints rose again on the day of our Lord's death. Matt. xxvii. 52, 53.

435. Will our bodies also rise again?

Yes, for He has said so who wakened Lazarus from the dead, who Himself rose from the dead, and through whom the bodies of the saints rose again.

436. Will these very bodies rise again, in which we are at present?

Yes, for otherwise there would not be a resurrection of the body, but a new creation.

437. Why does this mention of the Resurrection follow the Forgiveness of sins?

Because only those rise to *eternal life*, who died in the forgiveness of their sins.

438. And why does this have place in the Article concerning the Holy Ghost?

Because through the resurrection of the body the work of our sanctification is completed, which is begun in the forgiveness of our sins.

439. And what else do you believe in the Third Article?

The life everlasting.

440. Why does this come just after the Resurrection?

Because everlasting life, for which our bodies also were created, does not begin in its completeness until after the resurrection.

441. And why does everlasting life have a place in the Article concerning the Holy Ghost?

Because everlasting life is the final goal to which the Holy Ghost leads us through our sanctification.

XXIV.

442. Tell me whether, according to the Explanation of the Third Article of the Creed, you can come to faith in our Lord Jesus Christ?

Yes.

443. Can you also come to Him, and be united with Him in time and in eternity?

Yes, I can, I dare, and I ought to.

444. Can you do this of your own reason or strength?

I believe I cannot by my own reason or strength believe in Jesus Christ my Lord, or come to Him.

445. Why not?

Because of the sin born in me I lack light and power. Rom. iii. 11, 12.

446. Who gives you faith, and brings you to Jesus Christ?

The Lord, the Holy Ghost.

447. How does He do this?

In the order of salvation.

448. What is the first thing the Holy Ghost does in the Order of Salvation?

He calls me.

What is it, to call?

449. What has He called you from?

Away from the world and forth from the kingdom of Satan.

450. And what has He called you to?

To His Kingdom, His Church, the Holy Communion.

451. And how has He called you?

Through the Gospel.

What is the Gospel?

452. Why do you say, Through the Gospel, and not, Through the Law?

The Law commands, and because we neither

can obey nor answer, it threatens and curses us, and frightens us from God. But the Gospel forgives sins and promises life and peace to sinners, and so it invites and attracts us. No one comes for the Law's sake; whoever comes, comes because of the Gospel.

453. What is the second gift of the Holy Ghost?
He has enlightened me with His gifts.

What is it, to enlighten?
454 How does He enlighten us?
With His gifts.

455. And what are those gifts?
The bright light of the Law and the Gospel, and the knowledge that streams from both.

456. What light does He give you through the Law?
He enlightens me concerning myself, my wicked heart, my countless sins.

457. And what light does He give you through the Gospel?
He enlightens me concerning my redemption—concerning my Redeemer, and the salvation He has won for me.

458. And what does the Holy Ghost give in the third place?
Sanctification. He has sanctified me.

459. What does this mean?
He has separated me from the world and worldliness, and placed my feet on the way of peace and love, and given me both the desire and the power to go in this way.

460. And wherein does He sanctify you?

In the true faith.

461. Why do you say He sanctifies you "in the faith"?

Because without the faith there is no sanctification.

462. And why do you say, "in the true faith"?

Because a false faith cannot sanctify, whether it be that a man believes what is false, or on the other hand does not thoroughly and honestly receive the true faith. John xvii. 17; 2 Peter i. 5–8.

463. How can you attain the true faith?

Through the Gospel, which is the power of God unto salvation, Rom. i. 16. Through the preaching of faith, from which come faith (Rom. x. 17) and the Spirit also (Gal. iii. 2; Rom. v. 1ff.).

464. What is the last step or grace of the Order of Salvation mentioned in the Catechism?

Preservation. The Holy Ghost has sanctified and preserved me.

465. And wherein has He preserved us?

In the true faith.

466. Why must we be preserved in the true faith?

Of what use would it be to have begun in the true faith, if we are not preserved in it? Not that I begin my course, but that I finish it, brings me to the prize of everlasting life.

467. But why do we again say, in the true faith?

Because faith alone, the true faith, and standing and continuing in it, saves. Mark xvi. 16.

468. And how long must faith be preserved in us, and must we be preserved in faith, if we wish to be saved?

Until our end. Rev. ii. 10.

XXV.

469. Does the Holy Ghost give the benefits of salvation to you alone?

Not to me alone, but to the whole Christian Church on earth.

470. Why do you say "on earth?"

The Christian Church in heaven has received all the good gifts of this Order of Salvation, and no longer is in need of them.

471. And what, according to the Catechism, does He do for the whole Christian Church on earth?

1. He calls her;
2. He gathers her;
3. He enlightens her;
4. He sanctifies her;
5. He preserves her.

472. In union with whom does He preserve the Church?

In union with Jesus Christ.

473. And wherein does He preserve the Church?

In the one true faith.

474. In speaking of each of us, there is nothing said of "Gathering," but of the Church is said, "He gathers." Why is this?

Just as you would not speak of gathering

when you were bringing home single heads of wheat, but you gather many thousands of heads, so we say of the whole Christian Church, but not of separate souls, that He gathers them.

475. Ought not the Gathering be mentioned after the Enlightening, for must not one be enlightened before he can really belong to the Church?

Not only are the children gathered in Holy Baptism before they understand, but even grown people receive most of their Christian knowledge in the Church. The Church never waits for the perfect light before receiving unbelievers into her bosom. She gathers those who obey the call, in order that she may enlighten them.

476. The Holy Ghost is said to preserve the Church in union with Jesus Christ. Where is Jesus Christ?

Christ is wherever His Word is preached; and wherever any one through His grace believes His Word, there He makes His abode. Matt. xxviii. 18–20; John xiv. 23.

477. How then can we be assured that we abide in union with Christ and are preserved in union with Him?

When through His grace we believe His holy Word, and abide in this faith until our end.

478. You say, He has sanctified me in the true faith; of the Christian Church you say, He preserves her in the one true faith. Why do you use that word "One," in speaking of the Church?

It is clear without saying it, that I have but one faith. But it is worth saying and giving thanks for it, that the Holy Ghost brings so many men as are in the Christian Church to one faith and preserves them in the same.

THE CREED. 115

479. And why does the Holy Ghost bring men to one faith?

Just as there is only one Lord and God, and only one body, one Church, so there is only one true faith, and that faith only has the assurance of everlasting life. Eph. iv. 4–6.

480. What does the Holy Ghost do for you in this Christian fellowship?

He forgives my sins.

481. Yours only?

No. And the sins of all believers.

482. Why do you say, Of all believers?

Because the forgiveness of sins can be received only in faith.

483. How much sin does the Holy Ghost forgive you?

All sins; original sin and actual sins, sins of omission and sins of commission, old sins and new sins.

484. How often does He forgive you your sins?

Daily.

485. And in what measure does He forgive all your sins?

Richly.*

486. Through whom does He forgive you?

Through the word and ministry of reconciliation, 2 Cor. iii. 6; v. 18, 19; through His servants to whom He committed the Word and Ministry of reconciliation and of the keys,

---

* "*Daily, Richly,*" so does He care for our bodies in the First Article. Daily, richly, so does He provide spiritual food for the soul. My body and my soul rejoice in the Living God.

through whom He offers to His people calling, enlightenment, sanctification, and all spiritual blessings in this order.

487. Why do you say, "In which Christian Church," He daily richly forgives all my sins?

Because out of the Christian Church there is no forgiveness and no salvation.

488. What will the Holy Ghost do at the last day?

He will raise up me and all the dead.

489. Will not God the Son raise up the dead?

Yes. Like the Father raises up the dead, so does the Son, and so does the Holy Ghost. The Father wills; the Son speaks; the Holy Ghost performs. The resurrection is the one work of the Triune God. Rom. viii. 11; Ez. xxxvii. 5, 9, 14.

490. And when will this be done?

At the last day.

What is meant by "the last day?"

491. Will there be a last day?

The mockers say, "Where is the promise of His coming? But the Lord is not slack concerning His promise, as some men count slackness; but is longsuffering to usward, not willing that any should perish, but that all should come to repentance." 2 Pet. iii. 5–9.

492. When will the last day come?

"One day is with the Lord as a thousand years, and a thousand years are as one day."

THE CREED.

The day of the Lord will come as a thief in the night, unexpected, suddenly. 2 Pet. iii. 8, 10.

493. What conduct then befits Christians?

Watch, says the Lord, for ye know neither the day nor the hour when the Son of man cometh. Matt. xxiv. 42. We should eagerly expect and hasten unto the coming of the day of the Lord, in which the heavens shall be consumed with fire, and the elements shall melt with fervent heat. 2 Pet. iii. 12.

494. Will only believers be raised from the dead?

No. The Holy Ghost will raise up all the dead.

495. What will believers receive from the Holy Ghost at and after the resurrection?

He will grant me and all believers in Christ everlasting life.

496. And what will be the lot of those who die in unbelief?

They will receive eternal death.

497. Is there any likelihood that sometime there will be an end to eternal death?

No. Rev. xiv. 11; xx. 10, speaks of torment that continues forever and ever.

498. Why is not this spoken of in the Third Article?

Because it tells only the good gifts of the Holy Ghost, which His Church receives in this world and shall receive hereafter.

499. And how do we seal all that the Third Article and its Explanation say?

With a faithful Amen. This is most certainly true.

XXVI.

Justification by Faith Alone.

Although the term *Justification* is not found in Luther's Catechism, *justification* itself is found in every part of it. Whoever believes and has what the *Articles of the Creed*, and the *Parts concerning Baptism*, the *Keys*, and the *Lord's Supper* say, has enough; he is justified from his sins. But here, in praise and honor of the one true faith, of which the Explanation of the Third Article of the Creed has spoken, we wish to speak a little of the process of Justification of a poor sinner before God; and let the scholar mark it well.

It is a process, a trial in Heaven.

God is the Judge.

The accuser is our adversary, the devil.

The culprit is man.

The accusation is true; the conscience of the accused witnesses against him, and so does the Spirit, who searcheth all things.

The guilt is great.

The punishment is endless.

The Law is from Sinai.

The sentence is ready.

Then comes the Lamb of God, our High Priest and Advocate, with the Blood that speaketh better things than the blood of Abel. On behalf of the miserable, lost and condemned criminal, He urges His suffering and death in his place, His perfect merit and victory over all our enemies. What an advocacy! The poor sinner near to death embraces His feet, in fullest trust, and full of penitence and sorrow.

Then comes a voice from the Holy of Holies: Tear down the indictment. The guilty man is acquitted for Jesus' sake from all guilt and punishment; he is justified, and without price the righteousness of Christ is accounted his.

And what is done in heaven, on earth is proclaimed from pulpit and altar and in private absolution. It is forgiveness on earth as it is in heaven.

Now the poor sinner has all he needs.

Now, being justified by faith, he has peace with God (Rom. v. 1), and joy (Luke xv. 22, 24), and the joy of the Lord is his strength (Neh. viii. 10).

QUESTIONS INTRODUCTORY

TO THE LAST FOUR PARTS.

XXVII.

500. Of what do the last four Parts of the Catechism treat?

Of Means of Grace.

501. Of what Means of Grace?

1. *Of the Means of Grace* through which God offers Grace to us, and seals it.

2. Of the means by which man seeks and grasps the Grace which God offers to him.

Remark. Just as a beggar can get the gift offered him only by stretching out his hand to take it, and the giver puts out his hand to give it, so God's gifts are *given* and *taken*.

502. What is the means by which we seek and take Grace?

Believing prayer, of which Part III. treats.

503. And what are the divine means of Grace, by which God gives it?

The Word and the Sacraments.

504. Which Parts of the Catechism treat of the Sacraments especially?

The Fourth and the Sixth.

505. And what does the Fifth Part treat of?

The Word of God, the Absolution, or the Gospel of the forgiveness of sins.

QUESTIONS
INTRODUCTORY TO PART III.

506. What is the special subject of this part?
Prayer.

507. Does it teach us about prayer in general, or does it by an example of prayer show us how we ought to pray?
It shows us in the model prayer, how we ought to pray, and what we ought to pray for.

508. What is that model prayer?
The Lord's Prayer.

509. Why is it called "the Lord's Prayer?"
Because the Lord Himself taught it to His disciples.

510. Did they ask Him to do so?
One of His disciples said to Him, Lord, teach us to pray, as John also taught his disciples. Luke ii. 2.

511. What did the Lord answer?
He said to them, When ye pray, say, Our Father, etc., and taught them the prayer.

512. Did the disciples use this Prayer after they had it?
Undoubtedly they did; and not they alone, but for more than 1800 years it has gone up to

God from the lips of many thousands every hour of every day. It is the first prayer of Christendom, in the sound of which all the history of the world goes on, that never has been exhausted and never can be, and of which the oftener a man prays it the less tired is he.

513. How may we divide the Lord's Prayer?

The Introduction, the Seven Petitions, and the Conclusion.

514. What is the Introduction?

An address to God, such as must precede every prayer, though sometimes it may not be spoken. Ps. v. 1.

515. How may the Petitions be divided?

Into prayers and supplications.

516. Who has taught us to make such distinctions?

St. Paul, 1 Tim. ii. 1, admonishes us to make prayers, supplications, intercessions and giving of thanks for all men.

517. What do you mean by the distinction?

In one case we pray against an evil, in the other we ask a benefit.

518. In how many Petitions of the Lord's Prayer do you ask benefits?

In the first four.

519. What do you ask for in the first Petition?

That God's Name be hallowed.

520. In the Second?
For the coming of His Kingdom.

521. In the Third?
For the fulfilment of God's will.

522. In the Fourth?
For daily bread.

523. In which petitions of the Lord's Prayer do we pray against evil?
In the last three.

524. What do you pray against in the Fifth Petition?
Against the guilt of past sin.

525. And in the Sixth?
Against temptation to further sin.

526. And in the Seventh?
Against all consequences of sin, all evil.

527. How can you sum up the Seven Petitions?
Six petitions urge the greatest need of the soul, the first three the greatest benefits of heaven, the last three deprecate the greatest calamities, viz.: sin and all its consequences. And between these two sets of petitions is one which asks the supply of the daily wants of our bodies, our daily bread.

528. Are there any intercessions in the Lord's Prayer?
All the petitions are intercessions, because in each every one prays for all.

529. What is understood as "the Conclusion" of the Lord's Prayer?

According to the Catechism, the Amen.

530. But is not another Conclusion often understood?

Yes, the Doxology which is appended to the seven petitions, Matt. vi. 13, *For Thine is the Kingdom, etc.*

QUESTIONS ON PART III.*

XXVIII.

531. Repeat the Introduction to the Lord's Prayer?
Our Father, which art in Heaven.

532. How do we address God in the Lord's Prayer?
As our Father.

533. Why is the Triune God called, in the Lord's Prayer, Father?
Because those who thus call upon Him are to be His children.

534. Is it not in the sense in which God is called Father in the Creed?
No. There we confess by the name Father the First Person of the Godhead, in distinction from the Second, the Onlybegotten Son of the Father, Jesus Christ. But in the Lord's Prayer we do not distinguish between the Persons of the Godhead, but we call the Triune God Father, because in Christ Jesus He is *our* Father.

---

*Instruction in Part III. becomes difficult, if it be looked on only as matter for teaching. All that we should do is, to help the scholars a little, where they do not understand, and for the rest to let the glorious explanation of Luther have way. While not affording material for diffuse lectures, this Part is adapted to frequent repetition.

THE LORD'S PRAYER.   125

535. Where is our Father?

In Heaven.

536. But is He not present everywhere, and not in Heaven only?

He is everywhere present on earth, and so we confess in the Creed. But Heaven is His sanctuary and the place of manifestation of His glory, where we shall see Him face to face. Thither our hope turns; thither the Lord Himself turns our hearts and thoughts in the Lord's Prayer; and we look up and long and gladly pray, Our Father which art in Heaven.

537. But what is God's object in teaching us to pray thus?

He wishes to invite us to believe, who by nature neither believe nor trust.

538. And what does He invite us to?

To believe that He is truly our Father, and we are truly His children.

539. But is He truly our Father, and are we truly His children?

Are we not born of His Spirit? Are we not called by His Name (Is. lxiii. 16)? He is the Father of whom the whole family in heaven and earth is named. (Eph. iii. 15.)

540. And what ought we do, inasmuch as He is truly our Father, and we are truly His children?

Ask of Him.

541. And how ought we ask of Him?

With all cheerfulness and confidence.

542. What do you mean by "with all cheerfulness?"

Without fear or wavering.

543. And what, by "with all confidence?"

That we be certain He will hear us, and not doubt at all.

544. Tell me with what words does the Catechism briefly and well tell how we ought to ask of God?

As dear children ask of their father.

---

545. What do we ask for in the First Petition?

That His Name be hallowed.

546 And what Name should be hallowed before every other?

His Name *Father*, by which we address Him in the prayer Jesus taught us.

547. And what do you mean by hallowing His Name?

To keep it in our hearts apart from every other name, as the Name of the Most High, "to hold it holy and glorious as our noblest treasure and holiest possession," as the *Large Catechism* says.

548. But is not God's Name holy in itself; does it not belong to God, and in that very fact is it not separated from all other names and made holy and glorious?

Yes, God's Name is holy in itself.

549. What then do we pray for in the First Petition?

That it may be hallowed also among us; that by us also it may be exalted and honored above every name.

550. How is this done?

In two ways.

THE LORD'S SUPPER.

551. What is the one?

When the Word of God is taught in its truth and purity.

552. And the second?

And we, as the children of God, lead holy lives, in accordance with it.

553. And with what words does the holy Church pray for these two things in the Catechism?

This grant us, dear Father in heaven.

554. Why does the Church say this so earnestly?

Because it is impossible for a Christian to teach God's Word in its truth and purity, without mixture or addition, without the help of God—nor will he be able never to forget, but everywhere to show, that he is a child of God and therefore holy as his heavenly Father is holy, unless God help him thereto.

555. And how, on the other hand, is the Name of God profaned?

In two ways.

What is meant by "profaning the Name of God"?

556. What ways?

First, when any one teaches otherwise, and *Secondly*, when any one lives otherwise, than God's Word teaches.

557. For what does the Church of God pray therefore in the Catechism?

From this, *i. e.* from this profanation, preserve us, heavenly Father.

Remark.—Luther cannot forget in his Catechism that this

prayer begins, Our Father. Twice in the Explanation of the First Petition he names the Name, and calls upon it, while he calls us children of God. And in the *second*, *fifth* and *seventh* Petitions, and in the Explanation of the *Amen*, he mentions the lovely Name. And how like one, who had again become a child of God, the whole Explanation is!

XXIX.

558. What do we pray for in the Second Petition?

That God's Kingdom come.

559. Where is God's Kingdom?

In Heaven. There is Jerusalem, the free, the Mother of us all.

560. Wherein does the Kingdom of God consist?

In that everything is arranged under One Head, is inspired by the Spirit of the Head, and with one heart and voice worships and serves the Triune God.

561. Whither shall this Kingdom come?

It shall come down from Heaven to earth, that men also may be united under Christ, their Head in Heaven, and in one spirit, with one heart and voice, with the Church in Heaven, may praise and serve the Triune God.

562. Will all men be brought together to the Kingdom of Christ?

No. There will indeed be one flock and one Shepherd, but only a part of mankind will be gathered into the one flock; the others will not be God's flock, but will be scattered, and will wander away from Him forever.

THE LORD'S PRAYER.

563. But will the Kingdom of God really come on earth?

Yes. Its beginning is here already, wherever the Church of Christ is, and it will always continue to come, for God has undertaken it (Ps. lxxii. 8, 11, 17, etc.), and no one can hinder His works. God's kingdom comes indeed of itself without our prayer.

564. Why should we pray "Thy Kingdom come," if it comes of itself without our prayer?

Not merely because God wishes us to ask for what He has promised, but we are especially concerned lest God's kingdom pass us by, as it passes by many. We pray in this petition that it may come also to us.

565. What then is the meaning of "Thy Kingdom come?"

Come to us; stir up and increase Thy Kingdom, Thy Church, Thy people; spread it;* let it grow both inwardly and outwardly; let it ever become more Thine own, Thy Kingdom—subject and devoted to Thee—and forget not us who pray to Thee, and let us not be omitted from the number of those who are Thine.

566. How does God's kingdom come to us?

Before all, when our heavenly Father gives us His Holy Spirit.

567. Why do we need His Holy Spirit?

That by His grace we believe His holy Word.

---

* Here we pray for Israel and for the heathen. Let us never forget it.

568. And for what else?

That we may live godly here in time and in heaven forever.

569. But does all this result from the gift of the Holy Spirit?

Yes, where the Holy Ghost is,

There is Grace, for He is given to us out of grace alone;

God's Word, for He comes to us in the Word;

Faith, for from the Word comes faith, and through the Word the Holy Ghost begets it;

A holy life, for newness of life comes forth from the Word and faith;

And when this once begins, it never ends, but according to God's will it lasts here on earth and in heaven forever.

XXX.

570. What do we ask for in the Third Petition?

That God's will be done.

571. Where?

On earth.

572. How?

As it is done in Heaven.

573. By whom is God's will done in Heaven?

By the angels and the elect.

574. Wherein does the will of God consist?

In the fulfilment of the first two Petitions, in the hallowing of His Name and the coming of His Kingdom.

575. How does the Catechism describe God's will?

As His good and gracious will.

576. Why is God's will called "good"?

Because it intends nothing more than the hallowing of His Most High Name, and everything is good that serves that end, and on the other hand nothing is good that does not serve it.

577. Why is it called "gracious"?

Because all God's grace is found in His Kingdom and its coming, and His will intends nothing else than that the Kingdom of all grace should come to us.

578. Cannot this good and gracious will of God be done without our praying for it?

O yes, it is done indeed without our prayer.

579. For what do we pray in this prayer, then?

That it may be done also among us.

580. When is God's will done?

When God breaks and hinders every evil counsel and purpose.

581. What counsel and purpose are evil?

Such as would not let us hallow God's Name nor let His Kingdom come.

582. Whose will is of such a sort?

The will of the devil, the world, and our own flesh.

583. What do you mean by the world?

All men who do not with the Church hallow

the Name of God and strive for the perfect coming of His Kingdom.

584. And what do you mean by the will of the flesh?

The natural will of the unconverted, which has no pleasure in God and His will.

585. What do we ask God to do to this will?

Break and hinder it.

586. How can God break it?

When He does not let it be done.

587. When does He hinder it?

When He does not let it be attempted.

588. But what if, as often happens, the evil will continues?

We pray that God will strengthen and keep us.

589. What strength and keeping do we need in that case?

That we be kept steadfast in His Word and faith, that we may overcome the world, the flesh and the devil.

590. But, alas, we are variable, and easily fall from His Word and the faith?

We therefore pray that He will strengthen and keep us steadfast in His Word and faith.

591. Have we not reason to fear that if we live a long while we may ultimately fall from the comfort of the true faith?

Therefore we pray that He will strengthen and keep us steadfast unto our end, for until then we cannot be quite secure of our victory.

592. Have we good reason to believe that we are heard?

Yes, for he does not wish His Name to be hallowed for only a short time, and that His Kingdom should come for only a little while; but until the end and forever He wishes to keep us in the hallowing of His Name and in His Kingdom.

593. With what words does the Catechism confirm this?

This is His gracious and good will.

XXXI.

594. What do we pray for in the Fourth Petition?

For our daily bread.

595. Why is it called our daily bread?

Because it is given to us every day anew, and is given to supply the need of every day.

596. Why do we say, Give us "this day" our daily bread?

The meaning is, that we should expect and ask the supply of every day's need on the day itself.

597. And why?

Because we do not need it before, and do not know whether we will need it any longer than to-day.

598. Are we not permitted then to ask for daily bread for more than to-day?

Yes, but not with the confidence of the Fourth Petition, which the Lord Himself teaches us to say, and which we may confidently and joyously believe will be heard.

599. But does not God give to every one his daily bread, without our asking?

He does. God gives daily bread without our prayer even to all the wicked,* Matt. v. 44. All, both good and bad, stand in the benefits of His common love.

600. Why do we pray then?

We ask in this petition that He will lead us to acknowledge our daily bread, for they who pray for it more easily acknowledge it.

601. As what are we to acknowledge our daily bread?

We are to acknowledge it to be His gift, for which we ought to pray, that we may not take it as rude and godless persons take it from their parents, as if they were compelled to give it.

602. For what else do we pray?

That we may receive our daily bread with thanksgiving, for those who ask for it think it worthy of thanks.

603. Is it not enough to acknowledge that our daily bread is God's gift?

No, we should with thanksgiving confess that it is God's gift.

604. What is meant by "daily bread?"

All that belongs to the wants and support of the body, as the Catechism shows in detail,

---

*In the first four Petitions care is taken to show that all does not depend on our prayer. We pray for our own sake only, that we may not neglect God's good gift, but may receive it aright. To the humility of the high Giver should answer the prayerful humility of the poor recipient.

thereby agreeing with the explanation of the First Article of the Creed.

605. Does everybody have all that the Catechism mentions?

No indeed.

606. Why is it all mentioned then?

Not merely that we may know all we pray and give thanks for in the Fourth Petition, but also that every one, whether he have much or little, may know that it is God's gift and his daily bread, and may give thanks for it.

607. What do we ask for in the Fifth Petition?

For the remission or forgiveness of our sins.

608. And in what measure do we ask to be forgiven?

As we forgive those who trespass against us.

609. Can we forgive?

Yes, those who can truly say "Our Father," are God's children, are strengthened by their Father's Spirit, and are fitted for every good work, even to forgive.

610. Do we not in these words, "As we forgive those who trespass against us," offer God a price for forgiving us?

No child of God thinks that. In the Fifth Petition we pray for the stream of His heavenly forgiveness, and then we will let the thankful rivulets of this stream trickle upon our enemies. We are speaking not of a price offered for His forgiveness, but of a poor thank-offering of our hearts for the abundant forgiveness of God. Christians gladly forgive to the praise of our Merciful Father, but they always need anew the forgiveness of their own hearts. To let God forgive us and to forgive belong together.*

611. What do we pray for in the Fifth Petition?

That our Father in heaven will not look upon our sins.

612. What would be the result if He were to look upon our sins?

He would on account of them deny our prayer.

613. And why is our sin so great? and our prayer so weak?

Because through inborn sin we have lost all worth; we deserve nothing that we ask for; we sin much every day, and deserve nothing but punishment.

614. On what can we depend in our prayers, then?

On grace alone: that He will grant us all through grace.

615. But if God forgives our sins, and graciously hears our prayer, what does the Explanation, as well as the Fifth Petition, teach us to do?

To imitate the mercy of the Lord, and thankfully forgive.

616. And how are we to forgive?

From our hearts.

---

*If we can forgive, and do forgive, this is a proof that we are His, and that His Spirit has not forsaken us. This gives us confidence to come to God and ask Him again and again to forgive our daily sins of weakness. (See the *Large Catechism*, towards the end of the *Fifth Petition*.)

THE LORD'S PRAYER.

617. Is a hearty forgiveness a forgiveness in word alone?

No, we will heartily forgive and readily do good, to show indeed that we forgive.

618. Whom will we forgive?

Those who trespass against us.

Remark.—Very often a man injures his neighbor, and is angry against him, as if his neighbor were at fault. In such a case he owes not forgiveness, but an apology. This must be borne in mind.

XXXII.

619. What do we ask for in the Sixth Petition?

That God will not lead us into temptation.

What is it, to tempt? What is temptation?

620. Does God tempt?

God tempts no one.

621. But did He not, for instance, tempt Abraham to offer up Isaac?

Yes, but He tempted him to good, to a great proof of obedience, and not more than he was able to bear, as is evident. But in the Sixth Petition we speak of temptation to sin. And of this it is true, God tempts no one. James i. 13.

622. Why do we say, Lead us not into temptation, if He tempts no one?

Though He tempts us not, He could bring and abandon us to temptation of the devil, of the world, or of our own flesh.

What do you mean by "Flesh?"

623. Have any reason to fear this?

God might in wrath and just judgment

threaten us with it for our sins. 1 Kings xxii. 20ff.; 1 Chron. xxii. 1; Luke xxii. 32f.

624. What do we pray for then?

That He would guard us from the temptation of others, or keep us when it comes.

625. But since we know who our tempters are, namely the devil, the world, and our flesh, ought we not be able easily to avoid and escape from their temptation?

It is not so easy. For they deceive us; they disguise themselves; they make the evil they tempt us with seem good.

626. What will happen if we do not watch?

They will lead us away from the even path of the Holy Spirit to bad ways.

627. And what will the end be?

Misbelief, despair, and other shameful sin and vice.

What is Unbelief? What is Misbelief? What is Despair?

628. But since we are weak, and do not watch and pray as we ought, we certainly will be tempted often and sorely. What do we pray for accordingly?

We pray that though we be thus tempted, we may still in the end overcome, and have the victory.

629. What do we ask for in the Seventh Petition?

Deliverance from all evil.

630. What is this Petition called in the Explanation of it?

The sum of all; that is, it contains all the petitions. We are heard and blessed in all respects, when we are heard in this petition.

THE LORD'S PRAYER. 139

631. How many kinds of evil are mentioned in the Explanation?

Of body and soul, property and honor.

632. When is this Petition especially necessary?

When the hour of death shall come.

633. And why is that hour so serious?

Because in it we can once for all be freed from all evil, but as easily can be cast into the greatest of all evils, eternal death.

634. What more do we pray for at that hour?

That our Father in heaven will grant us a blessed end, and graciously take us from this vale of sorrow to Himself in Heaven.

635. What is meant by an "End?"

The end of this temporal life in this vale of sorrow.

636. And what is "this vale of sorrow?"

This sorrowful world.

637. What is the conclusion of the Lord's Prayer?

AMEN.*

638. How does the Catechism explain this?

Amen, Amen, that is, Yea, Yea; it shall be so.

639. What does this word of two syllables express?

It expresses the certainty that such peti-

---

* To whom does *Amen* belong in the Church, to the Minister or the Congregation? According to 1 Cor. xiv. 16, evidently to the Congregation. Compare Neh. viii. 6.

tions are acceptable to our Father in Heaven and are heard by Him.

640. On what is the certainty that our prayer is acceptable to God, grounded?

On the fact that God has bidden us pray thus. He cannot bid us do what is not acceptable to Him.

641. And what is the ground of the certainty that He hears us?

He Himself has promised to hear.

QUESTIONS
INTRODUCTORY TO PART IV.

XXXIII.

642. What is the subject of Part IV.?
The Sacrament of Holy Baptism.

643. What is a Sacrament?
A holy transaction, instituted by God, in which heavenly gifts are imparted through earthly signs, bringing the grace of the Gospel, *i. e.* the forgiveness of sins.

644. How many Sacraments are there?
Two, Baptism and the Holy Supper.

645 Does not the Roman Church teach that there are seven Sacraments?
Yes, Baptism, Confirmation, Penitence, the Mass, Marriage, Ordination and Extreme Unction.

646. Why then does the Lutheran Church acknowledge only two Sacraments?
Because the other five are not Sacraments in the sense in which Baptism and the Holy Supper are.

647. And why not?

Because they lack either the Divine command, or the earthly sign, or the heavenly gift, especially the gift of the forgiveness of sins, or several of these, or all.

648. In what sense could some of these be called Sacraments?

In so far as they are holy acts commanded by God. But then there would be more than seven Sacraments.

649. What is Confirmation?

A renewal and establishment of our baptismal covenant.

650. What marks of a Sacrament are wanting in Confirmation?

All. It has not the Divine command, nor an earthly sign, nor the promise of a heavenly gift.

651. Ought we not reject it then?

No. It is a beautiful and suitable ordinance of the Church from the beginning, which can bring a rich blessing through the Word of God used with it. Acts viii. 14–17.

652. What is understood by the Sacrament of Penitence?

The Absolution.

653. What is the Absolution?

The Impartation of the Forgiveness of Sins.

654. What mark of a Sacrament does it lack?

It has the Divine command and the heavenly gift, but not the earthly sign.

BAPTISM. 143

655. But is not the laying on of hands an earthly sign?

No, this is only a significant gesture or act, which confirms the words of blessing.

656. What more can be said of the Absolution?

It is most like the real Sacraments. (See *Apology*, 173).

657. Was it really instituted by God?

Yes. The Lord not only commanded that the Gospel should be preached to every creature, but He breathed upon His disciples and said to them, *Receive the Holy Ghost. Whosesoever sins ye remit, they are remitted to them; and whosesoever sins ye retain, they are retained.* John xx. 22, 23.

658. Why do you not call Marriage a Sacrament?

It has the Divine institution, though it does not belong especially to the New Testament, but it has not an earthly sign nor a heavenly gift. Gen. ii. 22ff.

659. What does Ordination lack?

Though based on Holy Scripture (1 Tim. v. 22), and rich in blessing, it has not an especial outward sign nor the promise of the forgiveness of sins.

660. And what is wanting to Extreme Unction, to make it a Sacrament?

Everything.

661. But does not St. James speak of it, James v. 14?

No; he speaks of an anointing with oil, but not of an anointing for death, nor of an anointing that would impart a heavenly gift, but of the application of oil for the cure of the sick.

662. Have Baptism and the Holy Supper the requisite marks?

Yes. With them we compare all the rest.

XXXIV.

663. What is the meaning of Baptize?

The Greek word from which our word *Baptize* is derived, means *to wash*.

664. Did they not at first dip under the water those who were being baptized?

Yes; but from the beginning those who were weak or sick were sprinkled with water; and for many reasons, especially in a more rigorous climate, the former custom was given up. Not the quantity, but the use, of water is commanded.

665. Answer me now from the Catechism. What is Baptism?

Water.

666. Is it water only?

It is not simply water.

667. What water is it?

The water comprehended in God's command.

668. What does that mean?

God has commanded us to take it.

669. Is it only comprehended in God's command?

It is connected with God's Word.

BAPTISM.

670. Say for me the command of God, in which the water of Baptism is comprehended?

Go ye and teach all nations, baptizing them in the Name of the Father and of the Son and of the Holy Ghost. Matt. xxviii. 19, 20.

671. Tell me the Word of God with which Baptism is connected?

The same words: I baptize thee in the Name of the Father and of the Son and of the Holy Ghost.

672. What does "In the Name of" mean?

By command of,

In the place of,

In confession and invocation of, the Triune God.

673. Can we baptize in God's Name, then, only when He commands it?

Certainly. We cannot do anything in the name of an earthly king, unless he has commanded it.

674. And must we confess and call upon God, if we would baptize in His Name?

Yes. For how could a man know that he was baptized in God's Name, if His Name were not mentioned, or confessed, or called upon?

675. But what is the most comfortable part of Baptism in God's Name?

That it is done in His stead, and therefore is as valid and effectual as if the Triune God were seen and heard doing it. (Tit. iii. 5–8; Eph. v. 26.)

676. Who has been commanded to baptize in the Name of God?

The disciples of Christ and the called stewards of the mysteries of God, to whom is committed the flock of Christ. 1 Cor. iv. 1; 1 Pet. v. 2.

677. But in a case of necessity may not another Christian baptize?

Yes, but only in a case of necessity.

678. Is it then permitted?

Yes, because all believers are a royal priesthood, and therefore in such an exigency have an equal qualification. 1 Pet. ii. 9.

679. Why then may they not baptize in any case?

According to the ordinance of Christ the call and the office are necessary to administer the Sacrament of Baptism. 1 Cor. iv. 1.

XXXV.

680. Should not every one be taught first, then baptized, inasmuch as this is the order of the words in the command?

All who are old enough, certainly should be taught to wish for Baptism for themselves. But even the Apostles did not require a long previous instruction of adults, and the words of our Lord in Matt. xxviii., rightly understood, do not require such previous instruction.

681. What do those words command?

They bid the Apostles make disciples of all peoples, baptizing and teaching them.

BAPTISM.

682. Why are children baptized before they can wish it or can come to it with a resolution of their own?

Because they also need Baptism (John iii. 5), and the Lord blessed them and promised them the Kingdom of Heaven, Mark x. If without instruction or a resolution of their own they can receive the kingdom of Heaven, why can they not in the same condition receive Baptism, and through it as a door enter into the kingdom of Heaven?

683. But if they have the kingdom, why do they need anything more?

The Lord does not say that the kingdom belongs to *all* children, but to *such*.

684. Are our baptized children such?

Yes, for the Lord Himself is at their Baptism as He promised to be (Matt. xxviii. 19, 20); to Him we bring the children in prayer;* and He receives and blesses them in His Baptism.

685. What is the blessing given in Holy Baptism; of what use is it?

It works forgiveness of sins.

686. And what more?

It delivers from death and the devil.

687. And thirdly?

It gives everlasting salvation.

---

* In the public prayers the Church prays for the children, even for the unborn, so that Mark x. 13ff., may comfort parents, even if their children die in their birth.

688. To whom does it give everlasting salvation?

To all who believe.

689. To all who believe what?

That it gives all this.

690. But what right have you to say it gives this to those who believe?

Because the words and promises of God declare it.

691. What words?

Those which Christ our Lord says in the last chapter of Mark: He that believeth and is baptized shall be saved; but he that believeth not, shall be damned.

692. But the children do not believe?

If that were so, they would not please Christ.

693. Why?

Because without faith it is impossible to please God. Heb. xi. 6.

694. But how can they receive faith?

He who promises the Kingdom of Heaven, gives faith to them, though in wonderful ways.

695. How do we know this?

For instance, St. John Baptist even in his mother's womb was filled with the Holy Ghost and rejoiced in his Saviour. Luke ii. 41, 44.

696. But how can so much be ascribed to Baptism? Does not Christ do it all?

Yes, *through* Baptism.

BAPTISM. 149

697. It is clear from Mark xvi. 16. that Baptism works the salvation of believers. But it says nothing about deliverance from death and the devil, and the forgiveness of sins?

One cannot be saved without the forgiveness of sins and deliverance from death and the devil. Acts ii. 38, 39; xxii. 16; 1 Cor. vi. 11.

XXXVI.

698. How can water do such great things?

Water cannot do them.

699. What does them?

The word of God.

700. What Word of God?

That which accompanies and is connected with the water.

701. What Word of God is connected with the water?

The words of institution, used and repeated in Baptism, and the promise from Mark xvi. 16.

702. What do we mean when we say the Word of God is with the water?

It helps the water to reach the end for which it is used.

703. Does the Word of God do such great things in all who are baptized?

No, only in those who believe.

704. What does the Catechism say?

The Word of God does it, and faith.

705. What faith is here meant?

That which relies on the Word of God which is in and with the water, that is, which gives restful assurance that all that God has promised to those who are baptized, will come true.

706. What if we were to use water only, and had not the command and promise?

It would be simply water, and no Baptism.

707. When is it a Baptism?

When with the Word of God.

708. How does the Catechism explain Baptism in this place?

As a gracious water of life and a washing of regeneration in the Holy Ghost.

709. Why is it called "a gracious water?"

Because through the promise of God it is full of grace.

710. And why do we call it "a water of life?"

Because, through the grace in it, it works life, imperishable, eternal life.

711. And why is it called "a washing of regeneration?"

Because it effects the new birth of the soul, while water is applied to the body.

712. And why do we say "in the Holy Ghost?"

Because only the Holy Ghost can impart to the water through the Word the power to help souls to the new birth.

713. Is not too much ascribed to Baptism in these words?

No, St. Paul says it. Tit. iii. 5.

714. But the Scriptures do not call Baptism a water of life: do they?

In this passage St. Paul says that the Holy Ghost is shed upon us abundantly through

Jesus Christ our Saviour, that being justified by His grace, we should be made heirs according to the hope of eternal life; and adds, This is a faithful saying.

XXXVII.

715. What does such Baptism with water signify?

It points to the death of the old Adam, or of inborn sin,

And to the quickening and resurrection of the new man, or of a new godly life.

716. How is the putting-to-death of original sin signified in Baptism?

The old Adam in us is to be drowned and die.

717. What is "to die?"

The old Adam with all sins and evil lusts.

718. And how is he to be destroyed?

By daily sorrow and repentance.

719. Is this accomplished once for all?

No, *daily* sorrow and repentance are necessary.

720. And how long must this continue?

As long as we live, for the old Adam does not die till our souls leave the body. Rom. vii. 24.

721. What is the use of Baptism then?

It assures us of the forgiveness of sins and of the power of the Holy Ghost for the battle of faith until the end. 1 Pet. iii. 21; Gal. iii. 26ff.

722. How does Baptism signify the awakening of a new life?

The water covers us like a grave; and we come forth like a dead man from the grave.

723. Who was buried in Baptism?

A dead man: one laden with all sins and evil lusts.

724. Who comes forth from Baptism?

A new man, who shall live before God in righteousness and purity forever.

725. What makes this great change?

The forgiveness of sins, the impartation of the righteousness of Christ and of the Spirit of sanctification, all given in Holy Baptism.

726. But why is it said that the new man must come forth daily, since one is baptized only once?

The old man does not die at once, neither is the new at once complete. The slaying of the old and resurrection of the new require therefore the daily renewal of our baptismal covenant, until the work shall be completed in death and we fully enter into eternal life. Eph. iv. 22–24; Col. iii. 9, 10.

727. What is the use of Baptism then?

It begins the quickening of the new man, and daily gives grace to put on anew the righteousness and purity of the new man.

728. What foundation in Scripture have we for this statement?

It is wholly taken from Rom. vi. 3ff.

BAPTISM.

729. Does the Apostle there liken Baptism to a burial?

Yes. He says, we are buried with Christ by Baptism into death.

730. Why does He say, "with Christ"?

Just as Christ was buried in expiation of our sins, so are we buried in Baptism, and His atonement is reckoned to us as if we were actually buried for the punishment of sin.

731. Does St. Paul also use the figure of a resurrection?

He says, Like as He was raised up from the dead by the glory of the Father, even so we also should walk in newness of life.

732. What does he mean by this?

Just as Christ victoriously came forth from His battle against sin and death and the devil, so should we, to whom His victory is imputed, live in holiness and joy as victors over sin and death and the devil, until our end, and forever.

QUESTIONS INTRODUCTORY

TO THE PART CONCERNING

THE OFFICE OF THE KEYS AND CONFESSION.

XXXVIII.

733. What do you notice when you look at the so-called Sixth Part in the Catechism?

That it is divided into two parts, marked A and B.

734. Why is this?

In order to mark the fact that the part marked A has been added to Luther's Catechism from the *Kinderpredigten of the Church Order of Brandenburg-Nürnberg of the year 1533.*

735. Why have we added it?

Although omitted from the *Book of Concord* of 1580, we keep it here, after the example of both old and new Catechisms, because it excellently completes the instruction of the Catechism.

OFFICE OF THE KEYS. 155

736. Of what then does this Part of the Catechism consist?

First of the words of Christ concerning the Office of the Keys, and then of Luther's example of how the simple are to be taught to confess.

737. And what is the subject of the whole?

The Office of the Keys and Confession.

738. What do you understand by the Call and the Office of the Keys?

The vocation and office of Pastors (Eph. iv. 11) and of Stewards of the Mysteries of God (1 Cor. iv. 1).

739. Why do you call this the Office of the Keys?

Because to the Ministry, according to the figure which our Lord employed, the Keys are entrusted. Matt. xvi. 19; cf. John xx. 21–23.

740. What do you mean by saying "To the Ministry the Keys are entrusted?"

The master of a house entrusts his keys to his steward, *i. e.* he gives him the oversight of his house, puts him over all that comes in and goes out, and over his stores and treasures. The keys always imply a certain authority. See Is. xxii. 21, 22.

741. If then the Lord says to Peter, I will give thee the Keys of the Kingdom of Heaven; what does He mean?

This means something like this: I will make thee a steward in my Kingdom, that thou mayest look after all that comes in and goes out (1 Cor. iv.), *i. e.* that thou mayest administer the treasures I have laid up for others, and that to every one of my people thou mayest give out of my riches what will answer to the needs of his soul. 2 Tim. ii. 15.

742. Did He give the Office of the Keys to Peter alone?

No. In St. John xx. 21–23, He gave it to the other disciples also, and to other ordained stewards.

743. But does He not, Matt. xviii. 15ff., give the Office of the Keys to the whole Church, and not to the ordained pastors alone?

He gave the Keys to the whole Congregation, for all the members dwell in his house, and everything is theirs, Keys, Office of the Keys, and Bearers of the Keys, Paul, Apollos, Cephas, all are theirs; given to them for their salvation and blessing and peculiar possession. Yet not all to whom the Keys have been given for a blessing are to bear the *Office* of the Keys, but only the called stewards and servants of Christ. 1 Cor. iv. 1.

744. What particular use of the Keys do we usually think of, when we speak of it?

The authority to forgive and retain sins.

745. And what phrase results from this?

We speak of *two* Keys, that which *looses* and that which *binds*.

746. Do men bind and loose with keys?

The iron bonds of prisoners are bound and loosed, shut and opened, with keys.

OFFICE OF THE KEYS.

747. Who are those whom these Keys bind and loose?
The children of men.

748. Are these in prison and in chains?
They are bound from their birth with the chains and bonds of sin and condemnation.

749. Who are loosed?
Those who, penitent, flee to the Gospel, and hunger and thirst after righteousness.

750. How are they loosed?
By the proclamation and impartation of the forgiveness of sins.

751. What name have we for this?
The Absolution.

752. Who are bound?
Those who persist in impenitence and sin in spite of all admonition, and despise the Gospel.

753. Does this refer to the Jews and the Mahometans?
No, they never were free. We speak here of the sinners and unbelievers who belong to the Church, and therefore once were free.

754. How are they bound?
By the proclamation, by authority of God and in His stead, that their sins are not forgiven, but they abide under the wrath of God, and are shut out from the congregation until they repent.

755. What name have we for this?
Excommunication.

756. What is the consequence of it?

An excommunicate person must be excluded from the Holy Supper until he repents, because he could receive it only to his condemnation.

757. Ought excommunication be pronounced hastily?

No. First we should observe the grades of admonition given by our Lord, Matt. xviii. 15ff. Only when this has been found fruitless, should we, according to the command of Christ, proceed to excommunication.

758. What is the consequence of the Absolution?

Free admission to the Sacrament of the Altar and to all of the Church's treasures of grace.

759. What then is the Office of the Keys?

A right division of the Word of God, through Absolution and Excommunication.

QUESTIONS

ON THE

OFFICE OF THE KEYS AND CONFESSION.

XXXIX.

760. Does the Office of the Keys rest upon an institution of God?

Yes, as is seen in the words cited from John xx. 21–23.

761. What did our Lord do and say to His disciples when He instituted this Office?

He breathed upon them, and said to them, Receive the Holy Ghost.

762. What did He then give to them?

With His breath He gave the Holy Ghost.

763. Why did He give them the Holy Ghost?

To forgive and retain sins.

764. What was implied in this Divine preparation for the forgiveness and retention of sins?

The commission and the command actually to forgive and retain sins.

765. This can be proven from John xx. 21-23. Show me how?

If it were not the Lord's will that His servants should forgive and retain sins, He would not have confirmed their forgiving and retaining beforehand, in the words, *Whosesoever sins ye remit*, &c.

766. Is it certain that this Office still continues?

As certain as it is that the Lord commanded to preach the Gospel, *i. e.*, Absolution and forgiveness, to all men. The Absolution is nothing else than the Gospel, only that it is the closest and loveliest application of it to individual persons. And it is obvious that the office, which even in the time of the Apostles belonged to others than the Twelve, 2 Cor. iii. 6; v. 18, 19; 1 Cor. iii. 5ff., has existed in the Church from the beginning until now.

767. But did not the Apostles differ very much from later pastors in their right to the Office of the Keys?

While they were greatly helped in this Office by their unusual gifts, yet the Absolution, and the refusal of it, is in the mouths of our pastors, as it was in the mouths of the Apostles, a Word of God the Holy Ghost.

768. But what if hypocrites are absolved because their pastors cannot see their hearts; or pious souls are excommunicated?

The guilt or responsibility does not cleave to the Pastor or to his Office, if he has erred through human shortsightedness. The hypocrite abides in his sin, and the unrecognized pious man abides in his peaceful conscience and in the peace of God.

769. How ought a Christian regard the office of the Keys?

He should believe what the called minister of Christ says to him.

770. When only should he thus believe?

When he deals with him according to Christ's Divine Ordinance.

771. When does this occur?

Especially when the called ministers of Christ exclude from the Christian Congregation open and impenitent sinners, and absolve those who repent of their sins and wish to amend.

772. Should all open sinners be excluded?

Those who repent should be absolved; but those are excluded who are impenitent.

773. Are all impenitent sinners excluded?

Impenitent sinners, whose sin is not open, cannot be excluded.

774. But what if the pastor knows the sin, and knows that it is not repented of?

Let him take the course advised in Matt. xviii. 15ff., and, if he sees it to be his official duty, withhold the Absolution and the Sacrament; but the formal excommunication is the climax of the course shown in that passage, by which the sin, at first known to but one or more, gradually becomes evident.

775. Accordingly, what sinners are loosed, or absolved?

Those who repent and purpose to amend.

776. Is it not enough to see that a person is penitent?

No. The sinner must express his purpose to amend that wherein he has sinned, and which he recognizes to be sin.

777. Why?

Otherwise his repentance is not pure.

778. When the Ministers of Christ act thus, what should we firmly believe?

That such a binding and loosing is as valid and certain in Heaven, as if our Lord Jesus Christ Himself had done it.

779. Where is the Absolution said?

In the Confession.

780. Do you think this extract from the Brandenburg-Nürnburg Kinderpredigten, 1533, gives too much to the Office of the Keys, to the injury of the congregation?

No. The ministers of Christ discharge their office in His Name, and therefore with Divine authority. Therefore they should never forsake the course laid down for them in Matt. xviii. 15ff. All they do, they do *with* the Congregation and *for* it.

XL.*

781. How many parts does Confession embrace?

Two.

---

*The Catechism of Luther is a real living churchly little book, because it teaches how the Church acts, confesses and absolves. This character is shown to belong to it beyond other Catechisms, by its *Table of Duties*, *Prayers*, and *Questions before the Communion*.

782. What two?

First, that we confess our sins.

783. And secondly?

That we receive Absolution or forgiveness from the pastor.

784. And how?

As from God Himself.

785. What will result, if we receive it as from God Himself?

We will in no wise doubt.

786. And?

We will firmly believe that through it our sins are forgiven before God in Heaven.

787. Does it make any difference whether we confess our sins before God, or before men?

In each case it is a different confession.

788. What sins should we confess before God?

All sins, even those which we do not discern.

789. Why?

Because we neither notice nor can perceive how often we come short, but God sees and remembers.

790. Where do we thus confess our sins?

In the Lord's Prayer. There we say, Forgive us our trespasses,—putting all our sins together, those we discern and those we do not know.

791. But what sins should we confess to our pastor?

Those sins only which we know and feel in our heart.

792. Must a man then confess to his pastor every sin of which he is conscious?

No, those only which he knows *and feels in his heart*.

793. How does a man "feel sins in his heart?"

They are hard and heavy, they cause anxiety and bitter tears, as is seen in the case of Peter, Luke xxii. 62.

794. Why should a man confess to his pastor the sins he knows and feels?

Because for them especially he needs the comfort of the Absolution.

795. But how can a pastor absolve, if he does not know all a man's sins?

He absolves in God's Name. God does it through him. God knows all a man's sins, and in Christ Jesus forgives even those which a penitent does not know. He knows the sin, the penitence and the faith, and will respect His absolution. For the pastor it is enough that he absolve no open and impenitent offender, and therefore does not share any one's sin and impenitence.

XLI.

796. If one wishes to prepare for Confession, what shall he do?

Let him consider his station.

797. What "Station" is meant?

The station of a father, or of a mother, or of a son or a daughter, of a master or a mistress, of a manservant or a maidservant.

798. And how shall you consider your station?

In the light of the Ten Commandments.

799. How is this done?

By answering questions suggested by the Ten Commandments. For instance, if you are a son or a daughter or a servant, have you been disobedient, unfaithful, slothful; or in general, have you wronged any one by word or deed.

800. And if on such an examination you find sins, which oppress you and you feel in your heart?

Then I may confess to my pastor what I know and feel, in somewhat the same manner as the example given in this book.

801. But what if you find no sin to accuse yourself of?

I will certainly always find more than enough.

802. We can however imagine men not knowing what to confess. What ought they do?

Let them beware of hypocrisy, and let them say the General Confession which it is customary to say to God in public worship, also to the pastor that he may absolve them.

803. How does this Part of the Catechism close?

With the beautiful formula of Absolution.

804. Is not this formula very short?

It is short, but it tells me all I can wish to know in the Absolution; so much that I could —if I were what I should be—draw strength and refreshment from it all my life.*

805. But those who have a heavy weight on their conscience, or are troubled and tempted: do they not need more?

The pastor will know well enough how to comfort such and bring them to greater faith, with additional words of God.

806. Could depressed, troubled and tempted souls keep to the formulas of the Catechism in their Confession?

Not easily. The heart will overflow, and they will find a way of confessing that needs no formula.

807. For whom then is the formula given?

For the simple, for those who do not know how to find a better way, but in all matters need to be told what to do.

---

*He who has forfeited his life, can get a pardon either in a long speech, or in the three words, Thou shalt live. Will he wish for a long speech, when he has heard the three words? Will they not be great and glorious to him, and sweeter than honey and the honeycomb?

QUESTIONS ON PART V.

XLII.

808. What is the subject of this Part of the Catechism?

The Sacrament of the Altar, or the Holy Supper.

What is an Altar?

809. Why is this Sacrament called the Sacrament of the Altar?

Because it usually is administered at the Altar.

810. And why is it called a Supper?

Because it is a meal, which in the first instance was dispensed by our Lord in the evening.

811. What does the Catechism say the Holy Supper is?

The Body and Blood of our Lord Jesus Christ.

812. Is there not perhaps in the Holy Supper only a symbol of the Body and Blood of Christ?

No. The Sacrament of the Altar is the *true* Body and Blood of our Lord Jesus Christ.

813. Why must this be said so earnestly?

Because the *Reformed* deny the presence of the true Body and Blood of our Lord in the Supper.

168 LUTHER'S SMALL CATECHISM.

814. Why do we not agree with the Reformed in this, it being so wonderful a thing that the Body and Blood of Christ should be wherever the Holy Supper is administered?

Because the Lord plainly said, This is my Body, This is my Blood.

815. But can the Body and Blood of the Lord be seen and tasted in the Supper?

No. His glorified Body and His precious Blood are, on account of our gross sins, not perceptible.

816. Where then are the Body and Blood of Christ to be sought and found in the Holy Supper?

Under the bread and wine.

817. What are the bread and wine therefore called?

The two *forms* or elements of the Body and Blood.

818. Are the bread and wine in the Holy Supper only visible forms, so that only Body and Blood are there, and not bread and wine?

No. Bread and wine are really there, are seen and tasted, and after consecration are called bread and wine by St. Paul. 1 Cor. x. 16, 17.

819. Does anybody deny that bread and wine remain in the Holy Supper, just as the Reformed deny the presence of the Body and Blood?

Yes. The Romanists say that in the Supper the bread and wine are changed into Body and Blood, and that of the bread and wine nothing remains but the outward appearance.

820. What do we say, inasmuch as we learn from the Holy Scriptures to acknowledge the presence of the Body and Blood, and also of bread and wine?

We say that the Body is united with the

SACRAMENT OF THE ALTAR.

bread, and the Blood is united with the wine, and therefore under the bread we receive the Body of Christ, and under the wine we receive the Blood of Christ.

821. Why are Body and Blood offered to us in the Holy Supper under the bread and wine?

To eat and to drink.

822. How do you prove this?

By the words of Christ, Who says, *Eat, Drink.*

823. If the Body and Blood of Christ are in the Holy Supper for us to eat and drink, for what purpose are they not there?

They are not there to be looked at, carried about, and worshipped, for they are not given for that.

824. To whom are the Body and Blood of Christ given to eat and to drink?

To us Christians.

825. How do we become Christians?

By Baptism and faith.

826. Can unbaptized persons receive the Holy Supper, then?

No.

827. Can unbelievers?

No. They are not Christians.

828. How can unbelief be detected?

If one openly professes that he does not believe in Jesus Christ, or if he indeed wishes to pass for a Christian but lives in stiffnecked impenitence and vice.

829. Are there not a good many who confess Christ, but are not His at heart, yet of whom it would be impossible to prove this?

Such are hypocrites, and they receive the Sacrament to their own peril.

XLIII.

830. Can we observe the Holy Supper with a good conscience? Ought we do so?

Yes, we ought. It was instituted by Christ for that purpose.

831. Who have told us about it?

The three Evangelists, Matthew, Mark and Luke, and St. Paul in 1 Cor xi.

832. When did our Lord institute the Holy Supper?

The same night in which He was betrayed.

833. What night was that?

The night between Holy Thursday and Good Friday; for then Judas had betrayed Him.

834. What did our Lord then do?

He took the bread.

835. What sort of bread was it?

Thin unleavened cakes, such as the Jews used in the Passover.

836. And what did He do, when he had taken the bread?

He gave thanks, as He always did before eating.

837. And then?

He brake the bread.

838. Did each disciple receive a whole loaf or cake?

No, each received a bit of the same loaf.

839. Did the disciples help themselves to the bread?

No, He gave it to them.

840. Did they receive it in their mouths, or in their hands?

We do not know, and it makes no difference. At any rate He gave it *for* their mouths, to *eat*.

841. What did He say?

Take, eat, this is my Body.

842. And therefore what, according to His own words, did He give with the bread?

His Body.

843. What Body?

The Lord said, My Body, which is given for you; therefore no symbol, but His true Body.

844. How could He do this when He was there before their eyes in the body?

That He could do it, we know because He said so. *How* He did it, is His care, not ours, nor do we know. It was however no greater miracle than He does now in distributing the Body in which He lives forever, to so many thousands of believers.

845 We receive the Body that was given for us. Why was it given?

To bear the punishment of death for our sin.

846. Why do we say it was given for us?

Because the Body of Christ was given instead

of, in the place of, our body, and therefore for our benefit. And in consequence, our body will not be punished.

847. Do we receive it to our benefit, in the Sacrament?

How can it be otherwise, if we are His disciples? John vi. 54.

848. Wherein does the blessing derived from the Sacrament consist?

If we receive with our mouths the Body that was given for us, we can no longer doubt, but we surely know, that it was given for us, and we are at peace with God. It is like the sacrificial meals of the Old Testament. We cannot doubt that the Sacrifice has been offered, if we eat of it.

849. What do we spiritually feed upon in the holy Body?

Complete peace in the Sacrifice offered for us, and forgiveness of sins, therefore eternal life for body and soul. John vi. 54.

850. What else did our Lord say after giving His Body to the disciples?

Do this.

851. What ought we do therefore?

Take bread, give thanks, break it, hand it, say what He said, and receive the heavenly Gift.

852. And why ought we do this?

In memory of Him, to show forth His life and suffering and death for us.

SACRAMENT OF THE ALTAR.

853. Is the Holy Supper therefore a Memorial of Jesus?

Most certainly it is.

854. In it do we commemorate Him only?

No, He remembers us and our need much more, and in the Bread gives to us His Body for the remission of sins. We remember Him in receiving the bread, and He remembers us by giving us in, with and under the bread His Body, that we may become members of His Body, His flesh and blood; and He gives to us forgiveness of sins, that body and soul may rejoice in the Living God.

XLIV.

855. What else did our Lord do after they had supped?

He took the Cup.

856. An empty cup?

No, it was filled with wine. He took the cup, because of the wine which was in it, which He wished to give.

857. And then?

He gave thanks, and gave it to His disciples.

858. And what did He say?

Drink ye all of it.

859. Why then do Romish priests not give the Cup to all Christians?

They say that our Lord gave it to His disciples only, and they were priests.

860. Are they right in this?

If they were right, the same reasoning would withhold the bread from the people.

861. Was the Cup withheld from the people in the time of the Apostles?

No. In St. Paul's 1st Epistle to the Corinthians it may be seen that the whole congregation received both the Body and the Blood, and we know that many centuries passed before the withdrawal of the Cup.

862. What was the reason for this?

The fear of spilling some of its contents.

863. Why is there no danger of spilling any of Christ's Blood?

Because the Almighty Lord unites His Blood with the wine which is *drunk*, but not with the drops of wine which are spilled. The error of the Romanists is a consequence of their wrong teaching that there is only Blood, and merely the appearance of wine, in the Holy Supper.

864. But how could they withhold the Cup from the laity without breaking our Lord's command, Drink ye all of it?

They argued that as no body is without blood, so the Blood of Christ is contained in His Body.

865. And what do you say of this argument?

The Lord, who is wiser than men, said, Drink ye all of it; and a servant ought not depart from His Master's word.

SACRAMENT OF THE ALTAR.

866. What did the Lord say of the Cup?

This Cup is the New Testament in my Blood, which is shed for you for the remission of sins.

867. What does New Testament mean?

New Covenant.

868. Was there an Old Covenant?

Yes.

869. Through whom did the Lord institute it?

Moses.

870. With blood?

Yes, the blood of beasts. Ex. xxiv. 4–8; Heb. ix. 19–22.

871. On what was the Old Covenant founded?

On the obedience of men to the Law which God had given.

872. And on what is the New Covenant founded?

On the perfect obedience of Christ, and upon His suffering and death. Heb. ix. 11ff.

873. What is promised and given us for Christ's sake?

The forgiveness of sins.

874. How does God keep the New Covenant with us?

By giving us the forgiveness of sins. Heb. x. 16, 17.

875. And how is it kept by us?

When we trust His forgiveness.

176 LUTHER'S SMALL CATECHISM.

876. How are we rendered certain of His forgiveness?

By receiving the Blood which was shed for the forgiveness of our sins.

877. Why thus?

Because we cannot doubt that we have reconciliation and forgiveness, if we drink the Blood that was shed for the forgiveness of sins. Heb. ix. 13, 14.

878. Why does Christ say of the Cup: This is the New Testament?

Because in it He gives the Blood of the Covenant, by the believing reception of which we set our seal to the Covenant which is established between the Lord and us by the shedding of His Blood. The Cup is called the New Covenant, because it renders us certain of our Covenant with God and confirms it, just as I can call a book my consolation, if I derive consolation from it.

879. What shall we do as often as we drink of the Cup?

Do it in memory of Christ.

XLV.

880. Which of the Words of Institution show us the benefit we derive from the Holy Supper?

Given and shed for you for the remission of sins.

881. What is given to us through these words in the Sacrament, if we hear them with faith?

Forgiveness of sins, life and salvation.

SACRAMENT OF THE ALTAR.

882. But these words speak only of the forgiveness of sins?

Where there is forgiveness of sins, there is also life and salvation.

883. Has every one who eats and drinks in the Sacrament life and salvation?

No. It is not the eating and drinking that does it.

884. Why not?

How could so little a human work bring eternal blessing.

885 How then do we receive this blessing?

Through the words that stand here: Given and shed for you, for the remission of sins.

886. And what do we therefore call these words?

The chief thing in the Sacrament.

887. But the Catechism says these words "which accompany the bodily eating and drinking," are the chief thing. Why?

Because without the Eating and Drinking there is no sacrament of the Altar, and the whole blessing of the Sacrament is lost. For the Lord said, Eat, Drink.

888. Do all who eat and drink, have what they declare and mean, namely the forgiveness of sins?

No, only those who believe these words.

889. And what of those who do not believe these words?

They receive the Body and Blood of the Lord without the forgiveness, life and salvation.

890. How do they receive the Body and Blood of Christ?
To condemnation. 1 Cor. xi. 27ff.

891. On what does all depend?
That we receive *worthily*.

892. Is this the same thing as to be worthy of the Sacrament?
O no. No man can be worthy of it, however holy he may be.

893. What is it then to receive worthily?
It is to receive it in a way that honors the heavenly Gifts and the Heavenly Giver.

894. And is this effected through fasting and bodily preparation?
No.

895. But may we not fast?
Who will, may. It is a good outward discipline, and is not to be rejected so long as too great value is not ascribed to it.

896. What does the Apostle say of bodily preparation?
Bodily exercise profiteth little. 1 Tim. iv. 8.

897. Is it of no use then?
Little is not nothing.

898. How can you see that bodily exercise is of some use?
By observing persons who use it, and again those who do not, who come to the Holy Supper without it, or even indulge their flesh on the day of the Holy Communion.

SACRAMENT OF THE ALTAR.

899. Who, however, is truly worthy and well prepared?

He who has faith in these words, Given and shed for you for the remission of sins.

900. And who, in spite of all outward preparation, is unworthy and unfit?

He who does not believe these words, or doubts.

What does "doubt" mean?

901. All in the Sacrament depends on the words, FOR YOU. On what IN YOU does all depend?

On Faith. The words "For You" require truly believing hearts.

902. But are not very many condemned, when we add that we may not doubt?

There is a difference between *doubt* and *doubt*.

903. What doubter is unworthy and unfit?

He who is willing to doubt. He who fights against doubt and tries in faith to overcome it, is one of the weary and heavy laden, to whom Christ says, Come unto me, and I will give you rest.

OF THE COMPREHENSIVE SUMMARY, RULE AND STANDARD, ACCORDING TO WHICH ALL DOCTRINES SHOULD BE JUDGED AND ALL CONTROVERSIES SHOULD BE DECIDED.

(From the Preface to the *Formula of Concord*.)

1. We believe, teach and confess that the only rule and standard, according to which all dogmas and teachers should be esteemed and judged, are nothing else than the prophetic and apostolic Scriptures of the Old and New Testaments, as it is written Ps. cxix. 105: "Thy Word is a lamp unto my feet, and a light unto my path." And St. Paul says, Gal. i. 8, "Though an angel from heaven preach any other Gospel unto you, let him be accursed."

Other writings, of ancient or modern teachers, whatever reputation they may have, should not be regarded as of equal authority with the Holy Scriptures, but should altogether be subordinated to them, and should not be received other or further than as witnesses, in what manner and at what places, since the time of the Apostles, the doctrine of the prophets and apostles was preserved.

2. And because directly after the time of the Apostles, and even in their lives, false teachers and heretics arose, and against them in the Church, *Symbols*, *i. e.*, brief, plain confessions, were composed, which were regarded as the unanimous, universal Christian faith and confession of the orthodox and true Church, namely, the *Apostles' Creed*, the *Nicene Creed*, and the *Athanasian Creed;* we confess them as binding upon us, and hereby reject all heresies and dogmas which, contrary to them, have been introduced into the Church of God.

3. Moreover as to the schism in matters of faith which has occurred in our time, we regard the unanimous consensus and declaration of our Christian faith and profession, especially against the Papacy and its false worship, idolatry and superstition, and against other sects, as the symbol of our time, viz., *The First Unaltered Augsburg Confession*, delivered to the Emperor Charles V., at Augsburg, in the year 1530, in the great Diet, together with its *Apology*, and the *Articles* composed at *Smalcald* in the year 1537, and subscribed by the chief theologians of that time.

And because such matters pertain also to the laity and the salvation of their souls, we acknowledge as Confessions the *Small* and *Large Catechisms* of Dr. Luther, as they are included in Luther's Works, as the Bible of the laity, wherein everything is comprised which is treated at greater length in Holy Scripture, and is necessary for a Christian man to know for his salvation.

In accordance with this all doctrines should be tried, and that which is contrary thereto should be rejected and condemned, as opposed to the unanimous declaration of our faith.

In this way the distinction between the Holy Scriptures of the Old and New Testaments and all other writings is preserved, and the Holy Scriptures alone remain the only judge, rule and standard, according to which, as the only test stone, all dogmas must be discerned and judged as to whether they be good or evil, right or wrong.*

But the other symbols and writings cited are not judges, as are the Holy Scriptures, but only a witness and declaration of the faith, as to how at any time the Holy Scriptures have been understood and explained in the Articles in controversy in the Church of God by those who then lived, and how the opposite doctrine was rejected and condemned.

---

*Accordingly the *Small Catechism* must be compared with Holy Scripture, that we may know that its teaching is of God.

BRIEF INSTRUCTION CONCERNING THE BIBLE, OR HOLY SCRIPTURES, THE PROOF OF OUR CONFESSION, AND OF ALL DOCTRINE.

1. *What is the Bible?*

It is the Book of Books, a collection of books given us by God the Holy Ghost, the written Word of God to mankind.

2. *Into what two parts is this collection of holy books divided?*

Into the Old and New Testaments.

3. *Why is it thus divided?*

God has made with men a twofold Covenant or Testament, the one with Abraham and his posterity that among all people they should be His own chosen people; the second, however, with all believing disciples of Jesus Christ gathered from all the nations of the earth, that they should be His own chosen Church. The former part of the Bible contains those divine writings which were written in the time of the Old Covenant and refer to it. To those which were written in the time of the New Covenant, is given the name of the New Testament.

4. *What books belong to the Old Testament?*

The books of the Old Testament were arranged in the times of Ezra (478) and Nehemiah (444) in three divisions, the Law, the Prophets, and the Scriptures. Under the *Law*, were understood the Five Books of *Moses*. Among the *Prophets* were the books of *Joshua, Judges, Samuel,* and *Kings,* and *Isaiah, Jeremiah, Ezekiel,* and the *Twelve Minor Prophets*. To the third division belonged, *Psalms, Proverbs, Job, Canti-*

cles, *Ruth, Lamentations, Ecclesiastes, Esther, Daniel, Ezra, Nehemiah* and *Chronicles.*

5. *Do we still divide the books in this way?*

No. We commonly speak of the *Historical, Poetical* and *Prophetical* Books, and divide them thus:

I. HISTORICAL BOOKS.

1. The five books of Moses, the *Pentateuch*, viz., *Genesis, Exodus, Leviticus, Numbers, Deuteronomy.*

The work of one man, except the little that Joshua or others may have added afterwards.

2. The book of JOSHUA.

According to chapter xxiv. 26, the work of Joshua except the conclusion, and some little additions which cannot have been written by him.

3. The book of JUDGES.

The writer is unknown.

4. The book of RUTH.

Written after the time of David, by an unknown writer.

5, 6. The first and second books of SAMUEL.

These are one. The division was made in the Greek translation called the *Septuagint*, and from it came into the Latin, the *Vulgate*, and into the Hebrew Bible. They have also been called the first and second books of Kings, and then four books of Kings have been spoken of. The writer is not known.

7, 8. The first and second books of the KINGS.

These also were not divided originally. They are both by the same writer, whose name is not known. Probably it was the prophet Jeremiah.

9, 10. The first and second books of CHRONICLES.

In Hebrew, *Annals*. Jerome uses the word, *Chronicles*. Written by a Levite, perhaps Ezra.

11. The book of EZRA.

Evidently by Ezra.

12 The book of NEHEMIAH.

By Nehemiah. Chapters 8-10 are ascribed to Ezra.

13. The book of ESTHER.
Writer unknown.

II. POETICAL BOOKS.

1. (14.) JOB.
Writer unknown.
2. (15.) The PSALTER or book of PSALMS.
Divided into five books (I. 1–41; II. to 72; III. to 89; IV. to 106; V. to 150). Collections of Psalms belonging to various periods, especially to the time of David.
3. (16.) PROVERBS.
A collection of Proverbs, in three parts: 1. to Chapter 9, collected by Solomon; 2. Chapters 10-24, with new title, *Proverbs of Solomon;* 3. Chapters 25–29, Proverbs of Solomon, which the men of Hezekiah, king of Judah, copied out, with two additions, *The Words of Agur,* Chapter 30, and Chapter 31, the words of *King Lemuel,* the *prophecy that his mother taught him.*
4. (17.) ECCLESIASTES, or the *Preacher.*
"The words of the Preacher, the son of David," (i. 1); but i. 12, says, I *was* king, as though a dead man were represented as speaking.
5. (18.) CANTICLES, the Song of Solomon.
6. (19.) LAMENTATIONS.
Five poems of JEREMIAH. 1. On the deportation and sufferings of the people; 2. On the horrors of the destruction of Jerusalem and the Temple; 3. On the sufferings of Jeremiah; 4. On the rigorous judgment of God, and the hope of better times; and 5. On the distress and shame of the people, with a prayer for restoration.

III. PROPHETICAL BOOKS.

1. (20.) ISAIAH, between Uzziah and the death of Hezekiah, 759–699 B. C.
2. (21.) JEREMIAH, son of Hizkiah, the Priest, of Anathoth in Benjamin. From the 13th year of the

INSTRUCTION CONCERNING THE BIBLE. 185

reign of Josiah until after the destruction of Jerusalem, 629–580 B. C.

3. (22.) EZEKIEL, son of Busi, the priest, among the captives carried away by Nebuchadnezzar with Jehoiakim, about 600 B. C. Lived near the river Chebar, which empties into the Euphrates at Carchemish.

4. (23.) DANIEL. In the 4th year of Jehoiakim (606 B. C.) taken captive to Babylon. Last prophecy of the 3d year of the sole monarchy of Cyrus (536 B. C.) (Witness of Ezekiel, xiv. 14, 20, xxviii. 3, and of our Lord, Matt. xxiv. 15.)

5. (24.) HOSEA, son of Beeri, under Jotham, Ahaz, Hezekiah, Jeroboam II. 69 years in the prophet's office.

6. (25.) JOEL, son of Pethuel. It is uncertain whether he was a contemporary of Amos, or lived later under Manasseh (700 B. C.).

7. (26.) AMOS, a shepherd of Tekoah, in the tribe of Judah, lived between the beginning of the reign of Jeroboam II. and the end of Uzziah's, 838–759 B. C.

8. (27.) OBADIAH. Prophesied against Edom, in the time of the destruction of the Temple (588 B. C.)

9. (28.) JONAH, of Gath-Hepher in Zebulon, shortly before or under Jeroboam II. 838–797 B. C.

10. (29.) MICAH, of Morescheth-Gath, under Jotham, Ahaz, Hezekiah, 758–699 B. C.

11. (30.) NAHUM, prophesied the fall of Nineveh, in the time of Manasseh (699–644 B. C.)

12. (31.) HABAKKUK, under Jehoiakim, prophesied against the destroyers, 610–509 B. C.

13. (32.) ZEPHANIAH, under Josiah, 641–610 B. C. Declared God's chastisement of Jerusalem and of her enemies, with Messianic prophecies for Jerusalem.

14. (33.) HAGGAI, born in Chaldea, encouraged to the building of the Temple. Second year of Darius Hystaspis, about 520 B. C.

15. (34.) ZECHARIAH, son of Berechiah. A contemporary of Haggai, like him encouraged to the building of the temple.

16. (35.) MALACHI, an unknown contemporary of Nehemiah. About 450 B. C., under Artaxerxes Longimanus.

6. *What books sometimes are placed between the Old Testament and the New?*

The *Apocrypha* or Apocryphal books, *i. e.*, such as, while they are good to read and useful, and always have been read in the Church, are not to be regarded as the Word of God, because they were not written by prophets, nor given by God, but all were written after the time of the prophets.

7. *Name the Apocryphal books?*

1. JUDITH.
Judith, a pious widow of Bethulia, a city of which we know nothing, kills a general of Nebuchadnezzar, named Holofernes, in the twelfth year of the reign of that king. The return of the Jews from captivity is here supposed to have occurred at a time before they had been led into exile. The book probably was written in the time of the Maccabees.

2. THE BOOK OF WISDOM.
The most beautiful of the Apocryphal books. The author is unknown. It appears to have been written in Alexandria, shortly before the coming of Christ.

3. TOBIT.
A pious Israelite of the tribe of Naphtali (of Thisbe in Upper Galilee) in 722 B. C., was carried captive to Nineveh by Shalmanassar. Having become blind in his 56th year, he receives sight again through his son. A fiction, of unknown date.

4. THE BOOK OF JESUS SIRACH or ECCLESIASTICUS.
A teaching of wisdom, modeled on the Proverbs of Solomon. Chapter l. 1-26, makes it appear as if Sirach were a contemporary of the High Priest Simon II. (217-196 B. C.) and had finished the book after the latter's death. The Greek translation, in which it has been preserved to us, comes from a grandson of the

author, and according to a not improbable tradition, dates from 131 B. C.

5. BARUCH.

Baruch, son of Neriah, Jeremiah's amanuensis, read this book before Jechoniah and other captives in Babylon in the 5th year of their captivity, and then it was sent to Jerusalem. Much that is in it cannot be reconciled with history. It certainly belongs to a later period.

6. THE TWO BOOKS OF THE MACCABEES.

The first book describes the war of the five sons of the priest Mattathias against the power of the Syrian kings, lasting forty years, 175–135 B. C. It probably was written 135–107 under John Hyrcanus, and in Greek. It is more worthy of belief than the *second* Book, which contains extracts from a history of a certain Jason of Cyrene relating to the deeds of the Maccabees. (176–161 B. C.) Probably written in Greek by an Egyptian Jew.

7. PORTIONS OF ESTHER.

In the Greek translation of the Bible these are interwoven with the book of Esther. They cannot have been composed earlier than 142 B. C.

8. SUSANNAH and DANIEL.
9. BEL AT BABYLON.
10. THE DRAGON AT BABYLON.
11. PRAYER OF AZARIAH.

All these are found in the Septuagint.

12. SONG OF THE THREE CHILDREN IN THE FIERY FURNACE.

Much used by the Church, in all times.

13. PRAYER OF MANASSEH.

Very beautiful. Found only in Latin.

8. Are these all the writings which are called Apocrypha ?

There are others; but these are all that were received in Luther's translation of the Bible, and are printed in some English Bibles.

9. Would it not be better always to omit them from the Bible ?

No. The Romanists hold these books as canonical;

the Reformed leave them out; the Lutheran Church, however, leaves them between the two parts of the Holy Scriptures, not as canonical Scriptures, but as useful and good to read, and as giving us information of the last four hundred years before Christ, of which otherwise we have none.

10. *What are the Scriptures of the New Testament?*
 1. The Four Gospels, and the Acts of the Apostles;
 2. The Epistles, or Letters, of the Holy Apostles;
 3. The Revelation of St. John.
Or, to mention the books separately:
 1. THE GOSPEL OF MATTHEW.

Matthew, or Levi, first a Publican or Tax-gatherer at the seat of custom near Capernaum on the Sea of Galilee, then an Apostle, wrote his Gospel first *for the Israelites*. According to old tradition, he was the first of the Evangelists to write.

 2. THE GOSPEL OF MARK.

Mark, or John Mark (Acts xii. 25; xv. 37), a relative of St. Barnabas, and according to old tradition, the companion and interpreter of St. Peter, is said to have written his Gospel after Peter's death, *for the Italians.*

 3. THE GOSPEL OF LUKE.

Luke or Lucanus, a physician, Col iv. 14, probably a Gentile-Christian, a companion and assistant of Paul, wrote (probably 64 A. D.) for a Christian named Theophilus, otherwise unknown to us, two books, to prove and confirm the instruction he already had received. These were this Gospel and the Acts of the Apostles. He writes for a Greek.

 4. THE GOSPEL OF JOHN.

John, son of Zebedee and Salome, the disciple whom Jesus loved, wrote his Gospel to contradict errors about the Person of Christ and His relation to the Father, probably under Domitian (95 A. D.) on the rocky isle of Patmos, not far from Ephesus, whither he had been banished. He wrote for the congregations of Asia Minor which he presided over, and sent it to them by the presbyter Caius.

INSTRUCTION CONCERNING THE BIBLE. 189

5. THE ACTS OF THE APOSTLES.
Embraces the period from the Ascension of the Lord to the close of the two years' imprisonment of Paul at Rome, 30–64 A. D.

6. THE EPISTLE OF ST. PAUL TO THE ROMANS.
Written at Corinth 57–58 A. D. Written to Rome, before Paul had been there.

7. FIRST EPISTLE OF ST. PAUL TO THE CORINTHIANS.
Written at Ephesus in 57. Corinth was the capital of Achaia, situate on an isthmus between Hellas and the Peloponnesus. There he had gathered a large congregation.

8. SECOND EPISTLE OF ST. PAUL TO THE CORINTHIANS.
Written in Macedonia, soon after the First Epistle, on a journey to Corinth, in 57, after he had received through Titus a report of the effect of his former letter.

9. THE EPISTLE OF ST. PAUL TO THE GALATIANS.
In Galatia, the northern part of ancient Phrygia, dwelt in Paul's time Jews, Greeks, Phrygians and Celts, among whom he had founded congregations in the year 52. To them he wrote this letter from Ephesus in 55, principally to show the relation of the Old Testament to the New.

10. THE EPISTLE TO THE EPHESIANS.
Ephesus, once the principal of the Ionian colonies on the Asiatic coast, some miles from the sea on the river Cayster, a meeting-point of the liveliest tendencies, where Greek æsthetic idolatry encountered Asiatic theurgy. Between 54 and 57 a congregation, composed of Jews and Gentiles, had arisen, prepared by Apollos, but founded by Paul. This letter Paul sent with the letter to the Colossians, by the hand of Tychicus, from Rome, about 61–63.

11. THE EPISTLE OF ST. PAUL TO THE PHILIPPIANS.
Philippi, originally a Thracian city built on the slope of a hill to the north of the Strymon and called

Crenides, united with Macedonia by Philip, the father of Alexander the Great, and settled with banished Romans by Augustus. The congregation gathered there by Paul consisted principally of Gentile Christians, and was the Apostle's crown and joy. From them he accepted support. Even to Rome they sent him assistance, through Epaphroditus, who then brought this letter back with him. 61-63.

12. THE EPISTLE OF ST. PAUL TO THE COLOSSIANS.

Colossæ lay in Western Phrygia, on the river Lycus. St. Paul was in Phrygia in 52 and 54, and perhaps founded the congregation then. Epaphras came to Rome to Paul, and brought to his heart grateful memories of the congregations of Colossæ, Laodicea and Hierapolis. Paul sent them this letter by Tychicus, with the letter to the Ephesians. 61-63.

13, 14. THE TWO EPISTLES TO THE THESSALONIANS.

Thessalonica, formerly called Thermæ, on the Thermæan Lake. A great commercial city, in which many Jews dwelt. The principal topic of these Epistles is the Second Coming of Christ. They are the first letters St. Paul wrote, from Corinth, in 53.

15. THE FIRST EPISTLE TO TIMOTHY.

Timothy, from a city of Lycaonia, probably Lystra, son of a Gentile father and a pious Jewish mother. He was a companion and a messenger of Paul. Paul intended him to be leader of the congregation at Ephesus, and this letter inducts him into that office. It is one of the last of Paul's letters.

16. THE SECOND EPISTLE OF ST. PAUL TO TIMOTHY.

Written from Rome shortly before the death of the Apostle.

17. THE EPISTLE OF ST. PAUL TO TITUS.

Titus, son of Gentile parents, companion and assistant of Paul. At the same time Timothy was sent to Ephesus, he was sent to Crete, to the same duty. Probably written between 64 and 66 from Macedonia.

18. THE EPISTLE OF ST. PAUL TO PHILEMON.

Tychicus, who was to bring Paul's letters to Colossæ

and Ephesus, was accompanied by Onesimus, who brought with him a letter from Paul to his master, Philemon. He was Philemon's runaway slave, had been converted by Paul at Rome, and the Apostle sent him back to his master, but asks the latter to set him free that he may use him in the service of the Gospel.

19. THE FIRST EPISTLE OF ST. PETER.

Simon, son of Jonas, a fisherman of Bethsaida on the Sea of Gennesareth, called by the Lord Cephas or Peter, and therefore Simon Peter. Pillar of the Church at Jerusalem. He died on the cross at Rome, June 29th, 67 or 68. This letter was written from "Babylon" between 64 and 67, to the Christians in Pontus, Galatia, Cappadocia, Asia and Bithynia, and sent to them by Silas, the assistant of Paul. A witness of the unity between Peter and Paul.

20. THE SECOND EPISTLE OF ST. PETER.

Written to the same persons. The farewell of the Apostle, who foresees his death, and once more raises his voice to warn against apostasy, error, and a denial of the judgment to come.

21. FIRST EPISTLE OF ST. JOHN.

Written without an especial address to his intimate Christians, his "Little Children." It refers to his Gospel, and may have been sent with it.

22. SECOND EPISTLE OF ST. JOHN.

Addressed to a Christian lady who with her children walked in the truth.

23. THIRD EPISTLE OF ST. JOHN.

To the presbyter Caius, the helper of the Apostle, probably the same that brought the *Revelation of St. John* from Patmos.

24. THE EPISTLE TO THE HEBREWS.

Written at the beginning of the Jewish War, about 64, to the believers in Jerusalem and Judea, who were in danger of apostasy, because in fear of suffering, and were tempted to it by the worship of the Temple. A triumphant comparison of the Old and the New Testaments.

25. THE EPISTLE OF ST. JAMES.

The author is the famous president of the Mother Church at Jerusalem, Acts xii. 17; xv. 13; xxi. 18ff; whom alone it befitted to send a letter to the twelve tribes scattered abroad. He calls himself "the brother of the Lord." Matt. xiii. 55; Mark vi. 6. (Acts i. 14; 1 Cor. ix. 5.) A James is mentioned among the brothers of Christ, whom antiquity assumed to have been sons of Joseph by a former marriage. Many think he was the son of the sister of Mary, herself named Mary, mentioned Mark xv. 40. Others think he was the Apostle James, son of Alphæus. Whoever he may have been, his Epistle is from the Holy Ghost, and does not contradict the doctrine of St. Paul.

26. THE EPISTLE OF JUDE.

The author is the brother of James. See Mark vi. 3. The letter assumes that James still is alive and probably was written about 60 A. D. An Apostle Jude is mentioned, Luke vi. 16; Acts i. 13, who in Mark iii. 18 is called Thaddæus, Matt. x. 3, Lebbæus and Thaddæus. In contents this letter resembles the Second Epistle of Peter, though it has peculiarities of its own.

27. THE REVELATION OF ST. JOHN. THE APOCALYPSE.

A wonderful and very edifying proclamation of the final lot of the Church of God, of which more has been said, written and debated than of any other book of the Bible. Its genuineness is testified to from the beginning, and it is a worthy finial of the Holy Scriptures. The holy Apostle and great seer of the New Testament received this revelation from the Lord Himself on the island of Patmos under the Emperor Domitian (according to Irenæus), or under Claudius (according to Epiphanius), and communicated it to the churches of Asia, and through them to the whole Church.

INSTRUCTION CONCERNING THE BIBLE. 193

11. *You have said that the Scriptures of the Old Testament were collected at the end of the time of the Prophets, in the days of Ezra and Nehemiah. Can we say the like of the Scriptures of the New Testament: that they were collected towards the close of the Apostolic age?*

We cannot. For the collection of the Old Testament were chosen the men of the Great Synagogue, especially Ezra and Nehemiah, who themselves had lived with Prophets and had received the Holy Ghost for their work. These highly-gifted men could do this work for the children of Israel; their position was such that they were sure of the confidence of their people. But the books of the New Testament were not given first of all to one people, and intended to be by them given to all nations, but had to commend themselves to the believers of all nations and by them be accepted as God's Word. To accomplish this there was no Synagogue, no Council—no single assembly of the Church had authority enough to commend the Scriptures of the New Testament to the whole Church as the very Word of God. This they did for themselves, and most of them did it from the beginning; and though questions were raised as to the divine origin of some of them, these were overcome, and after the first four centuries all of them have been acknowledged to be divine.

12. *You have spoken of a Divine gift of the Holy Scriptures. What do you mean by it?*

The sacred writers received the impulse to write in their office, as well as the impulse to speak, from the Holy Ghost (1 Pet. i. 20, 21). While they wrote, the Spirit of God kept them from error in telling that which they knew before—He wonderfully helped them to remember, so that they, as for instance, St. John in his Gospel, faithfully give the words of whole discourses of God, of Christ, and of His Apostles and Prophets, tell all the histories in right connection, and are able to set forth all according to God's meaning and purpose. The Holy Ghost also opened their eyes to know what they had not known before, revealed to them the future and led them into all truth. And in all cases He gave them for the right matter the holy and perfect word, so that they wrote and spoke in words, "as they were taught by the Holy Ghost." 1 Cor. ii. 13. This influence of the Holy Ghost upon the sacred writers we call Inspiration, and St. Paul himself witnesses, 2 Tim. iii. 16, that "all" or "the whole" Scripture is given by God. Compare 1 Cor. i. 2; 2 Cor. ii. 13; iii. 18.

13. *But is not the manner and style of every one of the sacred writers his own, and different from that of the others? If the Holy Ghost speaks through all of them, why is His manner of speech so various?*

It is one breath that sounds in the flute, the fife, the trumpet and the horn; but in the different instruments the one breath gives a different sound. So one Spirit speaks through all the holy men of God—the sense and contents of their words is one and is harmonious —but the manner and style vary, as in the case of the musical instruments. There is one Spirit, but a difference of gifts and tone—and this difference of tone is so much lovelier in the concord of the meaning.

14. *What do we call the whole of Holy Writ?*

The *Canon*, that is, the rule and standard of our faith.

15. *Can there be no other rule and measure for us, than the Holy Scriptures?*

No. As our Lord prayed in His high-priestly prayer, "Sanctify them through Thy truth; Thy word is truth," John xvii. 17. Only the truth can be our rule and judge, and the truth is God's Word, i. e., the Holy Scriptures.

16. *But do the Holy Scriptures contain all that God and Christ, the Prophets and Apostles, have said?*

No, of course not. The world could not contain the books that would be written, if it were attempted to set down all that Christ did and said. John xxi. 25.

INSTRUCTION CONCERNING THE BIBLE. 195

17. Could it be said then that the truth is not wholly given in the Scriptures, and that therefore they cannot be our rule and standard?

It would not be right to say so. If the word of the Old Testament is full enough to make wise unto salvation (2 Tim. iii. 15), how much more is the whole Bible of the Old and New Testaments.

18. You say that the Scriptures contain enough to make us wise unto salvation: but do they not then contain all that the Holy Ghost has said?

It is not necessary that they should; they contain enough, if they make us wise unto salvation.

19. Does not the Roman Church teach that there is another source of information, the tradition of divine words and truth handed down from mouth to mouth?

Yes, they put such a tradition side by side with the Holy Scriptures.

20. Has the Lutheran Church no respect for such tradition?

Yes, she respects every tradition, but she holds such tradition to be liable to error, and accepts it only when it agrees with the written Word of God; and if it tells something which the Holy Scriptures do not contain she does not dare to call it the Word of God. She tries tradition by the Word of God, and accepts no doctrine which is founded on tradition alone.

21. Is not the Lutheran Church in danger of rejecting much that is divine?

She can reject nothing helpful to salvation, so long as she accepts the Word which contains all that is necessary to salvation.

22. Did not our Lord promise to give to His Church His Spirit, who should lead her into all truth? John xvi. 23.

Yes, and the Church always has the Holy Ghost; but because a man can resist the Holy Ghost and wander from the truth, we are most certainly under His guidance when we simply cling to the certain written Word of God. The Lutheran Church, taught by experience, is afraid of error, and seeks the Spirit who leads into all truth in the Divine Word alone.

23. But are not the Holy Scriptures so hard to understand that we need tradition, or an interpreter sent or given by God?

I know that Romanists regard their pope as such an infallible interpreter, but it is as well known that the popes themselves often have erred, and that they can produce no promise of such an interpreter.

24. But does not the Bible need such an interpreter?

The Bible, of which St. Paul (2 Tim. iii. 15, 16) writes that it can make wise unto salvation, and that it is useful for doctrine, for reproof, for correction, and for instruction in righteousness, cannot be obscure.

According to Luke i. 4, Luke wrote his Gospel that Theophilus might know the certainty of those things wherein he had been instructed. Can the Gospel be ill-adapted to that purpose? St. Paul wrote a number of Epistles: is it possible that the congregations to which he wrote them could not be made wise by his words? Can the Scriptures fall short of their aim? Is it not true that is said in Ps. cxix. 104, 105, Through Thy precepts I get understanding: therefore I hate every false way. Thy word is a lamp unto my feet: and a light unto my path.

25. But does not 1 Cor. ii. 14 say, The natural man receiveth not the things of the Spirit of God: for they are foolishness unto him: neither can he know them, because they are spiritually discerned?

This does not say that the Bible is obscure; but that the *natural man* himself is in the dark. If he yield himself to the Word, it is clear to him, and the Spirit of God leads him from light to light. All depends on his not striving against it; then the Word gives him understanding and becomes a light to his feet.

26. Yet the spiritual man does not see everything, and it is undeniable that even the most enlightened men have not understood everything in the Bible?

True, yet it remains true that the Scriptures are clear enough to make wise unto salvation. It may be said that they contain three kinds of passages: 1. Those which are clear enough for any one to understand; 2. Those which are dark to all; and 3. Those which require study and explanation.

27. *How then shall a man use the Bible aright?*

First of all let him take hold of the first class of passages, those which are clear to all; and these are the most numerous. Let him be modest in reference to those which no one understands; and these are few. And in reference to the third class let him be modest, and abstain from passion, sinful excitement and prejudice, and he will go further and further into their sense, and will get more and more light.

28. *What does St. Peter say of the difficult passages?*

He says, 2 Pet. iii. 16, that in Paul's Epistles "are some things hard to be understood, which they that are *unlearned* and *unstable* wrest, as they do also the other Scriptures, unto their own destruction."

29. *What great help is offered to every right-minded and zealous reader of the Bible?*

The parallel passages, which are marked for us in the better editions of the Bible. That is, passages which treat of the same subject.

30. *How many kinds of parallel passages are there?*

Two, *Real* and *Verbal* parallels.

31. *What is the difference?*

Real parallels are such as treat of the same subject; *Verbal*, such as contain the same word.

32. *How far can such passages help us to a better knowledge?*

Scripture explains itself; what may be lacking in one place, is found in another of the same import.

33. *But after all industry in reading, prayer and comparison, are we not hindered by defects in the translation?*

Certainly we are; but the way of salvation is not

darkened in any of the great translations of Christendom.

34. Can you mention human means which render it easier to understand the Bible?

Biblical Geography and *Biblical Antiquities* will help us to understand the Scriptures in their connection and to see their great beauty and excellence. They will make much clear, definite and vivid, which seemed dark; and we will perceive the truth of what one of the church-fathers said, *Circumstances throw light upon words.* (Hilary.)

www.ingramcontent.com/pod-product-compliance
Lightning Source LLC
LaVergne TN
LVHW051555070426
835507LV00021B/2600